GABRIEL HEYMANS

The
Gold & Glory
of the
End-Time Church

Gabriel Heymans Ministries

1500 Beville Road 606-256
Daytona Beach, Florida 32114

Dedication

This book is dedicated to every born-again believer who aspires to be part of God's end-time revival of this last generation.

Furthermore, to my wife, Anita, for her patience, love, support and gigantic effort she contributed to the preparation of this manuscript. Also, this book is dedicated with sincere gratitude to Frank and Melissa whose obedience to God and financial contribution made this publication a reality.

Finally, I dedicate this book to the Lord, who has counted me worthy as His servant to entrust me with this wonderful message of revelation for the end-time church.

Contents

Introduction

The Christian message of provision, finances and wealth is certainly one of the most intriguing and important messages for the church world today. From the time of my baptism in the Holy Spirit in 1977 until the present time, I have embraced the message of prosperity as a personal promise of God to me, not only as a matter of faith, but rather because of God's great love for me and all of His children. In the early years of my ministry, I preached on the subject of prosperity regularly. However, in October 1986 the Lord clearly defined the particular type of ministry that He has called me to as "THE END-TIME MESSAGE FOR THE CHURCH." Subsequently, I have devoted my entire effort of ministry to the restoration of the end-time church and the final end-time world revival and har-vest that is to take place before the return of the Lord.

Since 1993, the Holy Spirit began revealing to me as I had never known before that the message of fi-nances and prosperity is part and parcel of the end-time message of the church, so that the great end-time spiritual revival of God's glory will run concurrently with an equally powerful revival of prosperity and wealth for the church. However, regardless of this new realization, I hesitated to put more emphasis on pros-perity in our ministry, simply because of the wealth of information that was already available on this subject.

In 1994 the Lord showed me that there is a great deal of difference between the message of "*biblical pros-perity for daily living*," as opposed to "GOD'S END-TIME MESSAGE OF PROSPERITY" for this final generation of the church. I saw this difference clearer than I see the faces of people! "THE EVERYDAY PROSPERITY MESSAGE" is God's will to prosper ALL Christians of ALL generations at ALL times, from the resurrection of Jesus to the rapture of the church! The "END-TIME MESSAGE OF PROSPERITY" on the other hand is some-thing entirely different. This message reveals a spe-cific strategy of God to "SHIFT" our planet's wealth from the ungodly to the Christians in this final generation. It is like a "BLITZ," a "SIEGE," a "QUICK RESHUF-FLING" of wealth, from the sinner into the hands of the church. This *end-time financial plan of God* should be understood as "A SPECIAL END-TIME PROPHETIC EVENT" scheduled to take place in conjunction with the final global outpouring of the Holy Spirit, to pro-duce God's end-time harvest of souls for the return of Jesus (James 5:7). The *financial revival*, and the *world harvest revival* of this final generation will both explode simultaneously, shortly before the catching away of the church. God's purpose for this last great revival of Christianity, is to save this final generation from the great tribulation that will come upon the earth after the church's departure to heaven.

Salvation through grace is now or never. We are rapidly nearing the end of the dispensation of grace. During the seven-year period of the great tribulation, salvation comes only through death and martyrdom. At present, grace is running out fast. But God has one final plan to bring *revival* to all people, as well as a structured financial plan to sponsor this end-time revival. This financial plan will carry a twofold purpose, namely: to restore the church to wealth and dominion, and to enable the church to finance God's great end-time global revival and world harvest before Jesus returns to catch His church away to heaven.

The purpose of this book is to focus upon the wonderful end-time "PROSPERITY VENTURE" of God, a venture which God has engineered so ingeniously, and with such great wisdom for these last days. This writing contains some specifics in the strategy of God, to equip and empower His poverty-stricken church suddenly with the riches of earth's resources of wealth. Once the wealth of the sinner has been transferred to the church, God's end-time army, "THE GLORIOUS CHURCH" (Eph. 5:25) will launch an invasion of salvation upon multitudes of lost peoples of the earth. This miraculous interchanging and exchanging of world finances between sinner and saint will take place so suddenly that the world scene will immediately be set for the final world harvest of lost souls. This miraculous event of prophecy, and the fulfillment of it, will mark the beginning of the church's final conquest, which will be the last successful attempt to fulfill the "GREAT COMMISSION" of the Lord Jesus.

Before we examine God's financial plan for the last days, let's talk about the importance of money in the church world, and its necessity to revival. This will help to clear up our Christian perspective of money, which must be sober and sound in order for us to under-stand how God wishes to prosper all of His people in these last days. The Gospel of the Lord Jesus is like a vehicle, whose mobility depends upon two crucial key factors. Without these two factors in place, the Gospel is rendered completely powerless and paralyzed. The Gospel vehicle, and its operation, controls the entire effort of the church in spreading the Word of God around the world. Let's consider the crucial message of the Gospel vehicle.

1 | The Gospel Vehicle

"Go into all the world and preach the gospel to every creature." Mark 16:15, NKJV

THE MOBILITY OF THE GOSPEL MESSAGE

The mobility of the Gospel message is like a motorcycle, which requires TWO wheels in order to function or run. One wheel spells immobility and is just as hopeless as none at all. The Gospel is also like the TWO legs of a man. Both legs are required to produce an athlete. One leg alone is as detrimental as none at all. Without both legs in place the person is handicapped and mobility is lost. The Gospel of Christ is the same, it requires absolute mobility, since it is destined to travel to all peoples. The "MOBILITY" of the Gospel depends totally upon the two "LEGS" of the athlete, or the two "WHEELS" of the motorcycle.

In order to preach God's Word to all nations, the Word has to be transported. The transportation of the Gospel is made possible through its "MOBILITY." The mobility of the Gospel is made possible through the "TWO WHEELS" of the motorcycle or the "TWO LEGS" of the athlete respectively, enabling it to be carried or transported throughout. Once full mobility is achieved, the Gospel can make its journey around the world. The two legs of the Gospel "ATHLETE" or the two wheels of the Gospel "MOTORCYCLE" in relation to the preaching of the Gospel are called "POWER" and "PROVISIONS." Without these two forces working together simultaneously, the Gospel vehicle is immobilized and suffers a breakdown and the Gospel athlete becomes incapacitated.

The Gospel of Power

The Gospel of Christ is the POWER of God unto salvation. It must be spoken in POWER, by someone who is anointed with Holy Ghost POWER, who subsequently must demonstrate the Gospel in POWER, with signs and wonders following the preaching. Without "POWER," the Gospel is simply another story which people choose to either accept or reject. The Gospel "POWER" is the first leg or the first wheel required for it to travel. THE POWER IS PARAMOUNT!

The Gospel of Provisions

The second leg or wheel to the mobility of the Gospel is "PROVISIONS." Call it donations, funds, support, finances, resources, money, or sponsorship, it is one and the same thing. Let's stop kidding ourselves, it is MONEY, hard CASH, GREEN STUFF. It is time we stop referring to money as finances, funds, contributions, collections, donations and what have you, and start calling it what it really is: MONEY!

2

When we relate to money matters in the church, we have this head in the clouds super spiritual attitude, almost pretending as if the money does not actually matter. But when it comes to everyday business situations, we quickly clear the cobwebs from our minds, screw our heads back on, and approach matters in a very levelheaded way. We know concerning financial matters of the world system, that the tax man does not ask for a contribution, he wants a certain amount of tax MONEY! The doctor, lawyer and landlord do not want a donation either, they want your MONEY for services rendered to you. Concerning financial matters of the church, let us use the same approach as we use in the secular world, by calling money what it really is: MONEY!

All people including Christians talk about money daily. In everyday life, and in the workplace, people deal with the issues of money in a realistic way. People work hard every day to earn good money for their families, besides, the end of the month always sneaks up on all of us quickly, and soon it is time again to pull out the money and pay all your bills with your own hard earned MONEY! We need to adopt the same sound attitude towards money in the church as we do in the secular world. Preaching the Gospel to the sinner around the world, paying our bills, and providing a good living for our families takes money! Family, bills, or the Gospel are all supported with the same commodity, "MONEY"! Plain, simple, natural, green paper money! Our every effort to spread the Gospel through preaching, printing, or promoting it to the world costs money. Every time we reach out to someone with the Gospel, someone has to pay for the cost involved. The Gospel is not supported through the Mafia or Hollywood, NO, Christians will have to do that. But the *non-chalant, not-important* attitude of many Christians towards money in general has brought poverty to many Christian households.

Subsequently, the SPONSORS of the Gospel are too poor to support the Gospel properly. Many dear Christians are still living on barely get-along street, and are trying to get along successfully without too much money. They are of the persuasion that the vow of poverty which they have taken sacrificially, will cause them to become very spiritual. However, it only causes them to be robbed of God's blessings of prosperity for them, and worse than that, they cause the Gospel vehicle to become immobilized, and the spreading of the Gospel to be stopped. Selfish self-centered believers such as these, who hide behind their doctrines of poverty, fail to realize that if someone else had used the same "crutch of poverty" which they are using as an excuse, the Gospel being unsupported would have failed to reach them, and they would still be lost in their sins. We need to realize that as Christians we are the only sponsors of the Gospel. Poverty pleading believers deny sinners the opportunity to receive the Gospel and be saved! The Gospel needs THEIR MONEY also as support before it can travel to the lost and dying people of the world. It is therefore evident that poverty curses both the Gospel as well as the individual Christian. However, the unsaved suffers the most loss as a result of poverty pleading Christians failing to send the Gospel on its journey around the world.

THE THREEFOLD CURSE

Poverty enforces a threefold curse:

1. POVERTY curses the poor with lack and misery.

2. POVERTY curses the Gospel with immobility! It silences the voice of God's Word.

3. POVERTY CURSES THE LOST WITH ETERNAL DAMNATION!! What a curse!

People usually look shocked when you tell them that the Gospel is not free, because they have been told all their lives that it is free indeed. But the Gospel is not free, the SALVATION of the Lord Jesus Christ is free, but the Gospel is not! God is self-sufficient, but the Gospel needs money as its SPONSOR to travel around the world to every person. As Christians, we are not part of the sin and slavery of the world system, yet we are still involved in the operations of the world system and its functions here on earth. For this reason we still have a need for natural things on earth, such as money, houses, cars, food, and other basic commodities of earthly life. We still live in a natural world with money as its financial mode of operation. Like it or not, believe it or not, we are still part of natural life on the earth, which includes the system of needs, desires, and provisions. The Apostle Paul tells us that God will supply all our NEEDS according to His riches in glory by Christ Jesus (Phil. 4:19).

We need to realize that God will use the "NATURAL RESOURCES" of the earth to meet all the needs of mankind in a glorious way. The natural resources of the earth in turn are represented, substantiated, and validated by one thing: "MONEY!" All of our resources and wealth are represented by money, which totals the sum of all earthly wealth. If this was not true, we would not need any money. But we certainly do, and so does the Gospel need money as its sponsor. When the sponsor fails, the Gospel is immobilized. It does not necessitate prayer to sponsor the Gospel. If it did, the millions of praying Christians would have accomplished the task already. It does not necessitate manpower either, otherwise the one billion Christians on earth would have been enough to accomplish the work already. Yes, surely prayer prevails, and it takes people to preach the Gospel, but the spreading of the Gospel takes money. That's astounding! But it is true! We have to realize this, once and for all. Let's settle it right now! Without money, there is no preacher, and no proclamation of salvation to the lost! Without money, God's Word has no voice, the lost hear no message, and the sinner has no chance to be saved! Nothing happens without the money! So the Gospel is not free.

We need to have our pockets lined with lots of money if we plan to go anywhere and be of much help to anyone. Airfares are not paid for in anointing or prayer, but with money. Commodities such as Bibles, food, supplies, equipment, tents, medicine, chairs, hospital beds, hotel rooms, and transportation (from a bicycle in India to a four-wheel drive vehicle in Africa), they all cost money, and are all purchased with the same means: money. That may sound terrible, but it's true! PEOPLE ARE COUNTED IN NUMBERS, BUT SOULS ARE COUNTED IN DOLLARS. The more dollars, the more souls. If you have a passion for lost souls you should have a passion for dollars, not in the sense of greed, but in the grace and love of God for lost souls. Someone might say, "That's ridiculous!" but really, that's realistic. Souls for God's kingdom are measured in dollars. Welcome to the real world. We have many people praying for the lost, and even more people who are willing to go to the mission field, but only a few of them have the money to do so. So all those many people who are called by God to go to the mission field don't get to go because they don't have the means to go. Subsequently, the multitudes of lost souls are not being reached. The point is that if we have all the money we need, we could reach the entire world in no time.

Let's ask the same question, slightly different now: "Is anything free anymore in the church?" Yes, there are some. Like old secondhand clothes donated to the church. "What about vehicles and equipment for the mission field?" Sure, some of these things are frequently received by the church as free donations, but they usually need fixing. And fixing or repairs costs money. So it all comes back to money again. If we hate money and shun it, we end up in poverty, and all our best efforts in the Gospel are stopped. The Gospel then becomes handicapped and immobilized, and does not accumulate any travel miles. In this event, the Gospel vehicle simply shuts down, because it is fueled by POWER and MONEY. Anyone who has money can become a sponsor of the Gospel. The bulk of the money of the world system is in the hands of the secular world (of people outside of the church), the sinner. And sinners don't sponsor the Gospel! They sponsor social events in society such as television programs, sporting events, political rallies and campaigns and what have you. The church on the whole does not possess much money, and because of that, many lost people die and go to hell, because they are not being reached. That is an awesome reality, but it's true. Without Christ people die and go to hell. But why does the salvation of so many people depend on us, the Christian community, you might ask? Simply because God has ordained PEOPLE with the COMMISSION to preach the Gospel. And we are supposed to preach the Gospel with a Bible in one hand, and money in the other hand; with miracle power in one hand, and lots of money in the other. Ironically though, while some factions in the church are still preaching poverty, and calling money evil, people are dying and going to hell all the time. You see, dear people, a lack of money and poverty in the church will make hell very rich. The only kind of riches or abundance that poverty can produce is "LOST SOULS IN HELL, WHICH IS THE DEVIL'S DAMNATION AND DEATH." POVERTY IN OUR POCKETS FILLS HELL WITH THE PERVERTED RICHES OF UNREACHED LOST SOULS!

For this reason, it is evident to me that the poverty doctrine in the church is a doctrine of demons (1Tim. 4:1). Poverty comes from hell, because it takes people to hell.

The Gospel utterly depends on POWER and PROVISIONS to fulfill its mission. Call them what you want, they remain the same.

Call them: POWER and PROVISIONS
                   MINISTRY and MONEY
                   MESSAGE and MEANS
                   SOURCE and RESOURCE
                   GLORY and GOLD
                   PATHWAY and PRODUCT

These two commodities of salvation go together like bread and butter, and milk and honey.

The PRODUCT is spiritual, the PROVISIONS are natural, and the RESULTS are eternal and irrevocable. These two forces work together to conquer and achieve success. They represent the greatest gift anyone can receive in this life — ETERNAL LIFE!

SOBER MINDED ATTITUDE

The time has come for us to change our thinking about the way in which we have preached the Gospel. We need to adopt a new SOBER MINDED attitude. It is time for us to approach money in a simple straightforward fashion, instead of the head-in-the-clouds-mystical syndrome. It is time to "ACCEPT MONEY FOR WHAT IT IS, AND USE IT FOR WHAT IT CAN DO!" That includes liking money, treasuring it, seeking it and accepting it as a gift from God; a priceless gift, for priceless souls of people.

The Gospel of salvation, irrespective of how spiritual and powerful it may be, is spread around through the world system of money and finances. A natural resource for the eternal source of life. However, by attacking the resource, the devil has attempted to put a stop to the spreading of the Gospel message primarily in two ways: The way of CHURCH POVERTY and the way of THE POVERTY DOCTRINES OF DEMONS.

1. THE WAY OF CHURCH POVERTY

Spirits of poverty have robbed the church of her resources from the very beginning. A general state of poverty has abounded in the church world from Pentecost until the present day. The Bible says that there is a way that seems right unto man, but the end of it leads to destruction. The way of poverty has been so destructive for the church over the last 2000 years. The church herself according to the Book of Acts is responsible for embracing poverty.

It is a hard thing to find poverty amongst the Jews anywhere in the world today, much less in the Bible. Yet in the Book of Acts, chapter 3, we find two Jewish Christians who had already forfeited their Jewish heritage of prosperity as the sons of Abraham. Peter and John are on their way to the temple, passing through the gate of the temple called Beautiful. In response to the lame man at the gate Peter says, "Silver and gold I do not have, but what I do have I give you..." (Acts 3:6). Amazingly, even Peter's Gospel vehicle had suffered a breakdown. Peter had the POWER, or the first wheel of the Gospel vehicle clearly intact, but he did not possess the PROVISIONS. The second wheel was already missing. In the early days of the church the Christians preached the Gospel with POWER and PENNIES. At least the early church had the POWER. Today the church has only PROBLEMS and PENNIES to preach the Gospel with, as opposed to POWER and PENNIES in the early church. The church has gone from POWER to PROBLEMS, on the spiritual side of things, but on the financial side, the PENNIES has always remained the same. POVERTY has always hounded the church.

How about this statement? "ALL CHRISTIANS ARE POOR!" Some Christians are aggravated at that and strongly oppose me for saying this. With a statement like that, it makes some Christians so mad that they oppose me with a vengeance! Some might even have a million dollars in the bank, or five, ten, maybe even more. "Well then," I would respond, "if you are rich, come with me to the country of India and let's take that whole nation for Jesus!" India comprises about 20% of the total world population or one billion people. But now we are talking too big for the church world. There are no Christians who individually possess that kind of money, especially to spend on the lost, neither are there any Christian organizations; Christian business group or Christian company that have the availability of billions of dollars to spend on winning the lost! That's the reason why I say that all Christians are poor; simply because we don't have the money to GET THE JOB DONE!

Don't count money in dollars, count money in souls. Don't measure your wealth in terms of a certain amount of money reserved in the bank either. NO! Measure your wealth in the ability possessed to reach the lost world with the Gospel. We, the Christian community of the world, can only consider ourselves wealthy when we possess the means to evangelize the entire world community with the Gospel. That is financial wealth! In the secular world the same is true, when the money is not available to get the job done you are still lacking irrespective of how much liquid cash you may possess. In the church world we should still consider ourselves poor because we do not have the money yet to fulfill the great commission. So we are still poor!

Consider the following statistic: The earth is presently occupied by almost six billion people. Approximately one billion of this number are already born again. Let us say that we are living in the kind of dream world which some factions of the church seem to portray in thinking that evangelism is cheap. They believe that winning a soul on the mission field costs only an average amount of ten dollars per person. But that is daydreaming. Simply unrealistic. A closer and perhaps more accurate estimate would be an average cost of perhaps a hundred dollars to evangelize each lost person on the mission field. At the end of the next decade, around the year 2010, which could possibly be the approximate time of the Lord's return, government agencies predict that the world population would have escalated to approximately ten to twelve billion people. Let's use some hypothetical figures to give us an estimate of what we are looking at regarding the end-time harvest. Let's assume that three billion are Christians by then (due to the normal regular growth of Christianity). Let's say that the world harvest will comprise 80% of the remaining number of nine billion people, which is 7.2 billion people. If approximately seven billion people are going to be reaped for God's end-time harvest, at a hundred dollars per person, the staggering estimate now totals over 720 billion dollars for the end-time world harvest, and all that would probably take place in an approximate seven- year period. OVER SEVEN BILLION PEOPLE AT A COST OF 720 BILLION DOLLARS OVER SEVEN SHORT YEARS! We are now looking at a very realistic estimated cost for the great end-time harvest of the Lord Jesus Christ!

Most Christians would respond to this calculation with a protest of IMPOSSIBLE, and a fivefold IMPOSSIBLE argument. IMPOSSIBILITY No. 1: The population estimate is too much. IMPOSSIBILITY No. 2: The harvest estimate is too much. IMPOSSIBILITY No. 3: The estimate cost is too much. IMPOSSIBILITY No. 4: The time frame is too short. IMPOSSIBILITY No. 5: The whole concept or idea is IMPOSSIBLE. Well, that is WHAT GOD LIKES TO DO! THE IMPOSSIBLE!

The present truth, however, remains. *The Church has ALWAYS been poor!* The secular business world controls all the money, and we in the international church community beg for a morsel of bread, by having cake sales, bake sales, rummage sales, yard sales, car washes, and what have you! We beg for pennies when we require billions, and we think we are doing great. It takes 25 years to finance a large new church facility, housing five thousand believers. But to build another *Mouse Park at Disney* takes a few days to produce the money that's required! Why the difference? Because the world has the money and we don't! They are rich and we are poor!

Whose fault is it that the church is poor? It's really our own fault. The church has been her own worst enemy. Don't blame someone else. Our own self-inflicted vow of poverty has prevailed against us for 2000 years. A strong poverty mentality has ruled the mind of the church for so long, that we don't even know what real money is anymore. In terms of quantity, we think FEW is a FORTUNE. We don't know how to relate the needs of a lost world in terms of money. We don't even realize what kind of money it will take to reap a world harvest of souls for the Lord! We simply don't know what money is anymore!

WHAT IS MONEY?

What is really money? How are we suppose to identify the true value of money? In the church world, we still measure money in terms of a certain AMOUNT of money, instead of relating it to what we need to COMPLETE THE JOB. We keep staring at FIGURES, instead of looking at the TASK that is set before us. As soon as Christians come into a little bit of money they declare the victory and get ready to retire. They think, "I have enough money now!" But they don't know what money is. Since the church has never had much of it, it's no wonder that we don't know what money is. Personally, for a long time, I never knew what money was either. But one day while I was watching a sports interview conducted on television, a boxing promoter told me what money was. When questioned about how much money he had made as a boxing promoter, he responded by saying, "AS LONG AS YOU CAN COUNT IT, YOU AIN'T GOT IT!" As long as you can count your money you really don't have any. What a visionary! There are many visionaries in the world of business, but in the church they are scarce. The financial vision of the average Christian family includes the needs of father, mother, the three kids, and enough left over for the family dog. That's all! Selfish and short-sighted.

The average Christian family vision consists of *PARENTS, PENNIES AND PUPPIES*, because we want to remain humble and poor for Jesus. God's vision for us on the contrary, consists of *MASSES, MIRACLES AND MILLIONS* (of dollars). How very contrasting in style, is God's vision compared to ours! How can we ever think that we are like God? We just want to make ENDS meet. But God wants us to go to the ENDS of the earth. We don't know what money is and we certainly don't know what God's plan is for us as His final *GENERATION OF GLORY*, concerning money and masses of people. As long as you can count it (money), you don't have it! Don't retire when you begin to reap some success. Keep going after more all the time, and remember that as long as you can count your profits, you have not arrived by any means. The church in these last days is going to need billions, not just a few dry bones! The world is waiting for us, and so is God, who has called us to go where the church has never gone before, and to do what the church has never been able to accomplish: THE FULFILLMENT OF THE GREAT COMMISSION!

2. THE WAY OF POVERTY DOCTRINES OF DEMONS

Religious spirits or demons, proclaiming their demonic doctrines of poverty, have bound the church up in a state of deception, making us believe that poverty is a treasure and a virtue in the kingdom of God. There are some of us who grew up in the church, and have been brainwashed since childhood, and we have become the product of a life of poverty lived in deception.

We need to realize that we are what we eat, and we have or become what we believe. We believe whatever we were consistently taught, so that we become the product of our doctrines and teachings. And this has been our downfall as Christians. Doctrines of poverty in the church have produced the kind of lack that we are facing today, and unless we change that, we will never be any different regarding prosperity. I believe that it is essential for us to have a funeral and bury the traditional source of our poverty before we can even begin to anticipate God's wonderful plan of wealth for these last days.

LET'S HAVE A HAPPY FUNERAL! DOWN WITH THE DEVILISH DOCTRINES OF DEMONS. It is DOOM'S DAY FOR DUMB DOCTRINES OF DEMONIC DISPOSITIONS! Let God's people go free!

Some of these doctrines might be as familiar as the family dog you used to grow up with. But be not fooled anymore. They are deadly enemies, which have enforced their grip of poverty upon Christians for many generations. We are indeed what we believe, and the stronghold of poverty doctrines in the church have produced the terrible fruit of poverty in our lives. It is time to get rid of these devils now! BURY THEM ONCE AND FOR ALL! They are destructive lies of poverty. Let's confront them and alienate them from our lives FOREVER!

POVERTY DOCTRINE NO. 1:
WORLDLY POSSESSIONS MAKE CHRISTIANS UNGODLY

"Possessions and material things will measure and shape your spiritual life," is what poverty preachers proclaim. "The more possessions you have the more ungodly you become," is their doctrine of belief. If this religious kind of reasoning was true, I suppose that the less possessions one has the more spiritual you become and the closer you walk with God. Then consequently every poor person must be a spiritual giant, and poverty-stricken areas like the continent of Africa for instance must be like a spiritual haven on earth. How absolutely absurd! If poverty produces spirituality, why did Jesus tell us to preach the Gospel to the poor? Natural possessions do not determine spiritual conditions of the heart. Our personal relationship and fellowship with God determines our spiritual state of life. Worldly possessions have nothing to do with a person's spiritual state of life. If sudden riches turn people cold towards God, they were never in love with the Lord anyway, but were just following God for what they can get out of Him. But material possessions have nothing to do with the spiritual life of God in us.

POVERTY DOCTRINE NO. 2: MONEY IS EVIL

The Bible says it is the "LOVE, LUST, OR CRAVING" for money that is evil. If money itself is evil, Christians commit sin when they receive a salary check. It will be an evil thing then to receive money in any way, form, shape, or fashion. Receiving offerings in church, or bringing any money into the church would then be a sin. Having any contact with money at all would simply constitute a sin for the Christian. If money is truly so evil, any dealings with it would be sinful. This is stupid. How then are we supposed to live? The poverty preachers say, "Well, of course we have to have some money to live on, but the less the better, because any surplus money leads to sin." That's hypocritical! If money is evil, then all of it is evil, not just some of it. And in order to keep yourself from evil, you will have to dispose of it all! No, money is not evil. The *lust* of money is evil. Many people have no money themselves, yet the money has them. The *love, lust and craving* of money is sin, but money itself is innocent. Imagine getting a handful of bills from the bank and then having to pray over it and sanctify it, because you do not know what this money was used for or what sins these bills have committed since they were printed. How absurd! Money is not evil! But lust is an evil and powerful force of destruction. The lust of money can be defined as the specific amount of money that a person can be bought for, or be willing to sell his soul for. For Judas it was 30 pieces of silver. The devil succeeded with Judas but the Lord Jesus could not be bought, because He did not have a price. Jesus did not come to be bought, but rather to purchase us from death. Nevertheless, money is not evil, it's a gift from God. Money represents the riches and abundant provisions of God. Every dollar should remind us of the goodness of God who gives us all things to enjoy.

Some people talk about "dirty money." They say that the money of sinners is dirty. Then if it is dirty, put it in the washing machine, clean it up, and put it to good use. "No, no!" people argue, it's dirty because it is used for evil purposes, to buy drugs, to commit prostitution, etc. Then take the money and use it for the right purpose that it may be clean. Some Christians would not receive money appropriated through some worldly means such as the lottery, or receive money from a beer company or a cigarette company, nor would they accept money donated to the church by a sinner. "That money," they say, "is unacceptable, because it has been defiled by sin." Therefore it is considered "dirty money." But the Bible says differently. The Word of God tells us that the wealth of the sinner (the so-called dirty money) is stored up for the righteous (Prov. 13:22). Now that's being BIBLICAL! What riches does the writer of Proverbs (Solomon) refer to here? The riches of money, the wealth of this world, and of the sinner. We need to realize, dear Christian, that money itself is a blessing, and that the paper money in our hands is neutral, until it is put to some use, whether it be good or bad. I recently heard a true story from a minister who told me of an interesting situation which had occurred with his father, who as an older minister, has served the Lord faithfully for many years in the ministry. The older minister had dreamt a strange dream in the nighttime, in which dream God had showed him a sequence of numbers of a particular lottery ticket. The incident startled him the next day, because he could still remember the numbers clearly. Being of the persuasion that the lottery is sin, he soon shrugged the incident off and pushed it out of his mind. To his utter amazement, however, the very next lottery drawing proved the number of his dream to be the winning number, with a price money of fifty million dollars! How shocking! Fifty million dollars! Just imagine what he could have done for the kingdom of God with fifty million dollars! But the opportunity was lost at that.

Now let's be sensible and mature about this. I am not telling everybody just to go out and buy lottery tickets relentlessly every week. But let's be open to the Spirit of God. Revealing the outcome of the lottery to His children is absolutely legitimate, and if God wants to use the lottery once in a while, He is entitled to do so! It was not the devil that did that, excuse me! If the devil could see the outcome of the lottery every week, he would give the hint to the worst satanist, and criminals, not a born-again Christian, much less a pastor. Since when is the devil going to help the people of God? That will be totally ridiculous! NO! God did that! "Why then?" you might ask. Because the wealth of the sinner is laid up for the just, as the wisest man of the Bible rightfully says in Proverbs. So, the Lord simply wanted to bless one of His faithful servants with a good retirement package! But unfortunately, the opportunity was lost. I wonder how much money the church has lost out on because of our ridiculously dumb doctrines, instead of embracing what is really scriptural and in line with God's will for our lives.

Religious concepts are hard to change. "Well, I won't take money from a sinner," someone still says. Well then you will always be poor anyway, because the sinners are the people who have the money. The church does not have too much of it. If you don't learn to receive money from the sinner or the world system you won't ever get too much of it. Besides, the wealth of the sinner is stored up for the righteous! That wealth is the so-called dirty money! God wants to give us all the dirty money of the dirty sinners, so that we can preach the Gospel to the dirty sinner, so that the dirty sinner may be washed and cleansed in the blood of Jesus, dirty money and all! The dirty money idea is just another lie of poverty, sold to the church by the devil! No! The money is not dirty, the devil wants you to believe that, so that he can keep you poor, and that he wouldn't have to pay back all the money that he has stolen from you. The devil owes you a lot of money, stolen away from under your nose, and as long as he can make us believe that all that money is dirty and unacceptable, he wouldn't ever have to pay it back to you, dear Christian. The devil cannot afford for you to learn the truth about the so-called dirty money. Oh no, you need to stand up and demand your money back. The devil is your thief, and if you find him now (which I sincerely hope that you do), he has to pay back sevenfold of what he has stolen! The devil has stolen our money! The so-called dirty money. The devil is holding on to your money and calls it dirty, but it is time for us to call it ours! Don't let him get away with it. Make him pay up in Jesus' name! And remember: it is not dirty money, it's only stolen money. The money of this world is not evil, it is good, and it belongs to the children of God. **MONEY is a GIFT FROM GOD!**

POVERTY DOCTRINE NO. 3:
POVERTY MAKES US HUMBLE

Humility is not a financial attribute, it is a spiritual one. Humility is cultivated in the spirit of man through fellowship with God. Humility is not produced through treacherous circumstances either. Most poor people are very proud anyway, they just can't AFFORD (financially

18

and circumstantially) to show it. On the contrary, if poverty makes us humble, rich people don't stand a fair chance to be humble individuals. So, God is punishing them for their wealth, instead of rewarding them. Someone may ask this question, "What if people seem to be humble, then acquire great riches, become arrogant, and drift away from God?" The truth is that their false humility soon vanishes after the money shows up and their dependence on God is no longer evident. They are still immature spiritually, and need to develop their spirit to greater maturity through fellowship with God, and meditation in His Word. But HUMILITY COMES BY WALKING CLOSE TO GOD, NOT BY WALKING CLOSE TO POVERTY. This is another lie of poverty, as usual, sold to the church by the devil.

POVERTY DOCTRINE NO. 4:
POVERTY IS THE PILGRIMAGE OF EVERY CHRISTIAN

According to doctrine, we are supposed to be a bunch of beggars, on a pilgrimage in a land that is not our own. Nonsense! The meek will inherit the earth, Jesus said (Matt.5:5). This planet was made for us. We are not paupers, we are PLANTERS of the kingdom of God, and REAPERS of God's harvest and prosperity. We sow in righteousness, and we will reap the fruit of the earthly AND the heavenly blessings of God in this life. We are not poor paupers, peddling up the hills of life. We are God's proud princes of life, prowling around to take the kingdom of God by force. God has given to us life, and breath, and ALL THINGS that pertain unto life and godliness. We are a PECULIAR people, a ROYAL priesthood (1 Peter 2:9). Have you ever found poor royals anywhere? Jesus is the King of all the kings of the earth. Poverty is as unbecoming to a Christian as if Prince Charles of England was living in a shack in the inner city somewhere in America. And we on the other hand are KINGS of a HEAVENLY KINGDOM, a royalty of far greater glory than any earthly kingdom such as the British monarchy or any other monarchy for that matter could offer. Poverty does not suit Christians, because poverty does not suit kings. This doctrine is just another lie of poverty. Christianity is the story of eternal riches, both natural and spiritual riches in the kingdom of God.

POVERTY DOCTRINE NO. 5:
POVERTY MAKES US GOOD WITNESSES OF JESUS

How can we be a witness and an ambassador for the King of wealth, the Lord of all prosperity, and be too poor to pay our bills? How can poverty be an asset of God's kingdom when the word "SALVATION" means wholeness of heart and fullness of life in every aspect, including financially. God's salvation fills our hearts with the RICHES of heaven, and the RICHES of God's grace. How then can we portray poverty, when the riches of the creator lives inside us. What a startling paradox that would be!

God's salvation in us will progressively produce corresponding fruit in our lives such as healing, health, prosperity, peace, and all the other benefits of God's covenant life in us. If God cannot even provide for me in my own personal needs, how will I convince the sinner to accept my God's salvation? How can God be good, but is unable or unwilling to make provision for His own blood-bought children? Didn't Jesus say that if we as natural parents know how to give good gifts to our children, how much more will our heavenly Father give GOOD GIFTS to us? How can poverty make God desirable to the lost? How can poverty accurately and truthfully represent the God of glory who has created all things? How can He be a God of splendour who lives in a throne room of indescribable beauty, but expects His children to suffer in poverty? How could we then appreciate the glory of heaven, where even the streets are paved with GOLD, yet the Lord is unwilling to share any of His riches with us? Besides, the world is filled with sinners who know that money is a good thing. They work themselves to death everyday to make more money, so that they may accumulate enough provisions for their needs. No way. Poverty is no tool for evangelism. Poverty is the most inaccurate portrayal of the Lord and His salvation. God is the possessor of heaven and earth and all things (Acts 17:25). He is the provider of all and the one who blesses all people! It is God's GOOD PLEASURE to give us His kingdom!

POVERTY DOCTRINE NO. 6:
POVERTY IS A BLESSING

This is just about the most stupid statement I have ever heard of in my life. I was raised in Africa, and was a firsthand witness to the horrors of poverty. I have seen starving black children with swollen bellies, dehydrated, malnutritious for months on end, laying on bare concrete floors in darkened old dilapidated huts, with no sanitation, no food to eat, no fresh or clean running water. There are no fresh supplies of any kind, and the poor locals are groaning in their sufferings; they have reached hopelessness and total despair in their inhumane circumstances, and are now preparing to face the inevitable: starvation and subsequent death.

I also remember doing some missionary work in the country of Botswana on one occasion. We would literally drive for miles on end, seeing only dead animal carcasses laying around in the dried up pastures, and when we finally reached the locals, their predicament was not any better either. I still recall vivid images from those experiences. I can remember how that the most intense hatred for the devil himself would well up on the inside of me, as I witnessed the horrors of poverty. I felt such overwhelming feelings of hopelessness, anger and total frustration, as well as such an awareness of compassion which caused me to weep uncontrollably at the sight of the inhumane suffering caused by poverty.

Poverty is a force of complete destruction, a force of death that will strip man of all his dignity, possessions, and all his self-esteem, until, humiliated and degraded to the level of an animal, he faces death with nothing left inside him. Poverty is the curse of curses upon the earth, even death is a whole lot kinder to mankind. Poverty produces a dualistic death, it murders people in two ways, from the outside and from the inside. Poverty kills man on the outside with hunger and starvation, and simultaneously kills him on the inside with degradation and humiliation. Before death finally sets in, the starving individual has become a skeleton on the outside, and an animal on the inside. Poverty is no blessing, it is a destructive force of hell. If poverty was a blessing, hell would be a paradise. What a lie of the devil this is! Poverty is a curse from hell, and God wants to deliver us from all the evil of poverty. Jesus died for it!

POVERTY DOCTRINE NO. 7:
WE MUST BE POOR LIKE JESUS

Religion has portrayed Jesus as some poor pauper who had no earthly possessions. But His garments were of such excellent quality that the Roman soldiers cast lots for it. Also, Jesus had a treasurer, Judas Iscariot, and he was stealing out of the treasury bag (John 12:6). Of course Jesus knew that, but Peter and John however, were unaware of it, otherwise Judas might never have had the opportunity to live long enough to betray Jesus. There was so much money in the bag that Judas' nasty habit went unnoticed. At the Last Supper, Judas proceeded to dip his bread in the same bowl with Jesus at midnight, whereafter he left the room immediately to betray the Lord. When Judas left so suddenly in a hurry, the Bible tells us that the rest of the disciples thought that Jesus had sent Judas out to distribute money to the poor! (John 13:29). Now wait a minute, this was back in the days before the existence of electricity, batteries, flashlights, cars, paved roads, street-lights, and any other modern invention. People did not travel much at night, except limitedly, and in very urgent situations. Yet Jesus had such a reputation as a giver that when the treasurer left the supper in such a hurry, and that too in the middle of the night, the rest of the disciples presumed that Judas would make a trip in the darkness without regard of the hour, in order to deliver some money urgently that could not wait until daybreak. WHAT A REPUTATION JESUS HAD AS A GIVER! Can you imagine any business, ministry, or church, opening their doors at midnight to write an offering check and then hand deliver that check at one in the morning, not willing to wait until dawn? And also to face the difficulty of doing this in the dark of night, with the inconvenience of dusty sand-filled roads and an oil lamp as the only light, casting only enough light to light up your footsteps ahead of you, as opposed to the modern means we possess today! Yet, with such a reputation of giving, Jesus' ministry had to be prosperous in order to keep on giving all the time. You cannot be a great giver unless you have great resources. Once He was nailed to the cross, Jesus became *"poor"* FOR US, so that by taking our poverty upon Him, He could redeem us from poverty. And on the cross Jesus experienced poverty for only a BRIEF period of time, once and for all, but not by having poverty forced itself upon Him, and lord it over Him. Oh no! Apart from this, Jesus was never poor and will never be poor, since the evil of poverty could never lord itself over the Lord of prosperity ever!

POVERTY DOCTRINE NO. 8:
POVERTY IS PART OF ONE'S SUFFERING

The Christian's heritage is one of wealth and prosperity. The Christian blessing of prosperity is a dualistic covenant blessing, old and new. To the Galatians, Paul says that Christ has redeemed us from the curse of the law, "...THAT THE BLESSING OF ABRAHAM

MIGHT COME UPON THE GENTILES..." (Gal. 3:14a). All the curses of the old covenant have been removed by Jesus' sufferings, but the blessings of Abraham have been passed on through the cross to everyone who becomes born again with the resurrection power of the Lord Jesus Christ. All the blessings of Abraham belong to the Christian, as an inheritance. By faith in Jesus, we are the sons of Abraham, and heirs of the promises of Abraham according to the promise (Gal. 4:26-29). All Abraham's blessings are mine in Christ, to the Jew first, but also to the Gentile who receives Jesus Christ as Lord and Savior. Partaking of the life of Christ in the new covenant makes us heirs of God and joint heirs with Jesus our Lord (Rom. 8:17). So the child of God has inherited a dual covenant of prosperity. It is a double barrel, twin turbo, power packed inheritance of heavenly PROSPERITY. God has made double sure that we do not miss out on the God-given opportunity of becoming prosperous. God has provided prosperity and wealth for us in both major covenants of the Bible, both Old and New Testaments.

POVERTY DOCTRINE NO. 9:
WEALTH AND GODLINESS DO NOT MIX

How absolutely absurd! God has created everything on planet earth, spiritual and material included. God has also blessed us with all "SPIRITUAL BLESSINGS" in heavenly places. These spiritual blessings in heaven are manifested on the earth as both spiritual and natural virtues. Even though the "ORIGIN" of all earthly substances began in heaven with God, these diversified provisions on earth materialize as natural blessings, even cars, houses and money, including the full spectrum of everything we have a need for, or may desire to have. God's blessings are truly every good and perfect Gift which comes from God above, and they are completely diversified, from the most spiritual revelation to the most natural material possession.

Solomon was the richest man in his day and was also the wisest of all, showing us the powerful mix of wealth and wisdom, material riches and heavenly riches together. The temple of Israel, which was the holy habitation of God, and the sacred sanctuary of the Jews, was a perfect blend of wealth and godliness, with all its gold and glory. Wealth and godliness mix together quite well. The mercy seat in the holy of holies for instance, was made of solid gold, with the actual "SHIKANAH" glory of God descending from above, until it rested in midair, inches away from the golden mercy seat, encompassed by the two golden cherubim angels, at the end of both sides of the mercy seat. (The message of the gold and the glory will be discussed in detail in chapter 4.)

God spoke through the prophet Haggai and said that the silver and the gold belong to Him. And what about the heavenly streets of gold in a place as spiritual as heaven? All I can say is, "Don't be ridiculous, devil, the spiritual things of God and the natural wealth of the world are a perfect blend, and go together like bread and butter." We don't have to make a choice between WEALTH and GODLINESS. God has given us both together in one PACKAGE DEAL OF SALVATION.

POVERTY DOCTRINE NO. 10:
WEALTH CAUSES US NOT TO TRUST IN GOD ANY LONGER

First, how are we ever going to become rich as children of God without learning to trust in the Lord in our daily walk? God's prosperity comes only God's way. If we deviate from trusting in God after He has made us prosperous, we are stupid and deserve to lose it all again. This may happen, though, if we take our eyes off God, and begin to trust in our newfound riches. The Lord's eyes are our eyes. If you take your eyes off the Lord, you are blind and will surely stumble and fall, and miss out on the rest of God's plan for your life. Do not trust in wealth and do not allow yourselves to be led by anything other than the Lord Himself in the affairs of our lives. Let us not worship the blessing, but the one who BLESSES, and keep our eyes on the Lord, instead of trusting in earthly wealth.

LET'S CLEAN HOUSE

Many other lies of poverty exist in the church world, but the ones we've just discussed represent the most prominent shackles of bondage that have kept the church in poverty for almost 2000 years. Let us strip away every lie of Satan concerning poverty, and LET US CLEAN HOUSE, TODAY! Let's begin to clear our minds of this poverty mentality that is so prevalent in the church. It is time for God's oppressed people to go free!

Let us look at the blessing of the Lord for His beloved church in these end days of insurmountable glory, which this final generation of the church will possess, enjoy and use, to deliver a great end-time harvest to the Lord at His coming in the near future. The blessings of the Lord await us now, as we shall see in the next chapter.

2 | The Blessing of the Lord

*"The blessing of the Lord makes one rich,
and He adds no sorrow with it."* Proverbs 10:22, NKJV

I do not think that anyone could argue with the simplicity of this Scripture. The blessing of the Lord under discussion here does not refer to spiritual things; no, it is simply MONEY! Spiritual riches have no sorrow to add to anyway, because they are straight from heaven! Solomon is talking about wealth and money, and he is speaking from experience. He was the richest man of his day and he teaches that it is neither man nor the devil who makes one rich, but only GOD. Second, Solomon tells us that the riches which God gives are a blessing, and not a curse. Prosperity is a GOOD thing. Third, Solomon concludes by saying that God adds no suffering or sorrow with the wealth that He gives you. God's wealth given to us is a pure and wonderful blessing.

The blessing of the Lord in these last days is like a financial investment account. Throughout the past 2000 years this account has been drawing interest, and now that the church has entered her final generation and hour, the entire account with all its accumulative interest will pay up in "ONE BIG LUMP SUM TO THE CHURCH." There will not be another generation of the church after us to reap the rest or the leftovers. The investment account situation was part of God's plan and wisdom for the last days of the church. We don't know exactly when the return of the Lord will take place, but it is no more than 20 years and probably no less than five years until His glorious return. This final generation must make a clean sweep of the end-time harvest and conclude God's 2000-year plan with the church shortly.

God's end-time plan of financial blessing through the church will be such a magnificent revolution of prosperity that it will stun Christians and shock the world. The vastness of this financial plan is inconceivable, however, I would like to share with you a portion of this enormous end-time financial plan of glory. The Word of God says that we know in part, and we see in part. Therefore, allow me to show you the part or portion of God's plan of prosperity for the end-time church that the Lord has shown me. The church is awaiting a glorious revolution of wealth and prosperity in the very near future, destined for this final generation.

The plan of the forthcoming financial revival which the Lord has shared with me is so astoundingly glorious and magnificent that it is hard for the natural mind to grasp at first. But what a wonderful plan it is! The church is about to be delivered from her 2000-year affliction of poverty, spiritual as well as material poverty. So great will the blessing of the Lord be upon us in these last days that the world will envy us and seek to share some of the vastness of wealth which we would have received from God!

God's financial plan of revival for the last days consists of five miraculous events or divine works, which God Himself will sovereignly perform in order to restore the church to financial glory. Jesus will soon return for a church which is glorious in every aspect of life. The earth and all its wealth will be shaken, released and transferred to the church in order to revolutionize the world financially and fulfill the prophecies of the last days concerning God's beloved church. What glorious times are awaiting us in the very near future!

A Fivefold Multiple Blessing

This fivefold miraculous financial plan of God for the end-time church can be summarized as follows. There will be:

1. A supernatural INCREASE in the house of the Lord.

2. A supernatural INHERITANCE for the household of God.

3. A supernatural EXPERIENCE in the house of the Lord.

4. A supernatural ENDEAVOUR for the household of faith.

5. A supernatural REGENERATION in the household of the Lord.

We may describe the five financial wonders mentioned above as follows:

1. The supernatural increase is a supernatural blessing upon the work of our hands, which

means that God will increase our profits in our profession or business, in an extraordinary way in these last days, resulting in supernatural INCREASE.

2. The wealth of the sinner has been stored away for the righteous for many centuries. In these final days of the church, all that wealth belonging to the unrighteous will be spectacularly and miraculously transferred to the household of the Lord, the church, thus resulting in a supernatural INHERITANCE for the people of God.

3. The coming together of the GOLD and the GLORY of God in the house of God in these last days is the fulfillment of another prophetic wonder, destined through prophecy for the end-time church. When the outpouring of the Spirit upon all flesh takes place in this time, the glory of God's presence will literally fill the house of the Lord, thus restoring the very glory of God to the church (see Eph. 2:19-22). Once the glory of God has taken up its rightful place in the church, the gold or wealth will find its way back into the church as well. So the wealth will come in through the PRESENCE and GLORY of God, thus the wealth is released through God's anointing, which is the supernatural EXPERIENCE.

4. The Lord will share some innovative ideas in business with His people in these last days, through the creativity and ingenuity of the Holy Spirit. These supernatural ideas may be as simple as the idea of making a hamburger, yet they will be successful enough to generate millions of dollars in profit, to support the ministry of the end-time church. This venture is called God's Holy Ghost hamburger idea, which,

when embarked upon by the individuals concerned, will become a supernatural ENDEAVOUR in the end-time church.

5. The miraculous biblical event of the multiplying of our existing human resources is probably the most spectacular miracle of all miracles. This incredible event will be in frequent manifestation by the power of God in these last days all over the world. It will release an indescribable and unlimited source of wealth for the church, a degree of wealth not previously known to mankind, but predestined by God to be manifested in these last days. This outstanding miracle of wealth is called the supernatural REGENERATION of human resources.

This fivefold financial plan of glory for the last days of the church on earth begins with a "SUPERNATURAL INCREASE" upon the works of our hands as the first of five glorious events, and as we progress throughout all five of these glorious events, we will notice that from one event to the next, there will be an increase in the power of God, and its miraculous performance and creativity, escalating from event number one to event number five, one after the other.

THE ABUNDANT BLESSING

The vast amounts of money which God will bring into the hands of the church in these last days will be mind-blowing. In this prophetic final hour of the church it is a matter of now or never. It has to be done now, and soon. The time is short. The hour is critical. The Holy Spirit is waiting and revival is ready to sweep into all the earth, as God's end-time harvest is waiting to be reaped before the return of the Lord. So the money is going to flow and the miracles are going to mount,

31

and the souls are going to be saved by the billions! Within the next few years we will arrive at this exact critical prophetic moment of time, when God's miracle plan suddenly explodes all over planet earth. This is the moment and hour that we were born for. This is the moment all of us have been waiting for in our hearts. This is the hour of divine destiny for our generation. The moment of God's glory through the final day, church. As we enter into this explosion of wealth at this critical moment of time so ordained of God, the blessing of the Lord will come upon God's people in a mighty way. All we will have to do then is for each one of us to be faithful to God in what He calls each one of us to do in this hour.

GOD'S HANDIWORK

The miracle of this fivefold multiple blessing of God's financial explosion for the church is going to be God's doing, it will be HIS HANDIWORK, a sudden, sovereign and supernatural manifestation of God Himself. This end-time financial work of God will be likened unto the days of Israel in the wilderness and the miracle manna in the desert. As long as Israel was obedient to God in their quest for the promised land, the manna kept raining out of heaven. As long as the church sets out to reap the great end-time harvest globally, in these last days, the financial miracles will continue to rain forth like manna from heaven. God sent the manna down in the wilderness. Where did it come from? How did He make it? How did the manna actually rain down from heaven? How did it happen so consistently every day? The answer is...GOD! God did it then, and He will do it now! He did it back in the desert, and very soon, He will do it again, this time all over the world!

What I wish to do in this chapter is to give you an idea of how the blessing of the Lord of which we are already partaking of daily is going to ESCALATE in our lives in these last days because of the urgency of the hour and God's plan for this final hour. Every financial blessing of the Word of God promised to us will inevitably be MAGNIFIED and INCREASED in an astounding measure during these last days of the church on earth.

The blessing of our labors is the first of five supernatural events which will mark the beginning of God's financial plan to restore the wealth of the earth back to the church. The blessing of God, the increase of our produce, or the works of our hands, is the first blessing of the fivefold financial plan of God. This first step of God's plan has to do with our occupation, career, and work situation. The anointing of the Lord will come upon the hands of the body of Christ which will release a supernatural increase of productivity and performance, success and blessing in the workplace. The Christian work force will mount up some astounding profits and increases in their work situation, which supernatural success will result quickly in tremendous professional favor and rapid promotion for God's people. Christians will simply outperform nonbelievers at work, and the power of God in operation in them will produce almost superhuman results of efficiency and success. Believers will produce the kind of success in weeks and months that is usually associated with years of successful progress. The WORK of our HANDS shall be blessed supernaturally. Believers will soon be promoted throughout the land to supervisory or leadership positions, finding the church in charge of the secular workplace, instead of the unbeliever. It will be a quick shift of power in the secular world, from the sinner to the saint. Suddenly, all business decisions will be made by Christians listening to the advice of the

Holy Spirit, instead of following their instincts. Just imagine what radical changes this will bring about in society, all of this happening in just a short space of time.

We are heading for a revolution of righteousness in the economy of the world! God will do a quick work and have all His people placed in the strategic positions of society, able to enforce God's will upon society in an instant. The release of this fantastic miracle upon society could come at any time in the near future, since the time is getting very short. With all of this in mind, we should familiarize ourselves with the blessing of our hands as described for us in the Word of God. We need to know what God is about to do for us. Let's look at the blessings of the Word of God briefly concerning the work of our hands, as we prepare for a huge flood of blessings that will rain down upon us in this final hour of glory!

THE BLESSING OF THE RIGHTEOUS

"The Lord will COMMAND the BLESSING on you in your STOREHOUSES and in all to which you SET YOUR HAND, and He will bless you in the land which the Lord your God is giving you. The Lord will ESTABLISH YOU as a holy people to Himself, just as He has sworn to you, if you keep the commandments of the Lord your God, and walk in His ways. Then ALL peoples of the earth will see that you are CALLED by the name of the LORD, and they shall be AFRAID of you. And the Lord will GRANT you PLENTY OF GOODS, in the FRUIT of YOUR BODY, in the INCREASE of your LIVESTOCK and in the PRODUCE of your GROUND in the land of which the Lord swore to your fathers to give you. The Lord will open to you His GOOD TREASURE (storehouse), the heavens, to GIVE THE RAIN to your LAND (business, etc.), in its SEASON (prophetic hour), and to BLESS ALL THE WORK OF YOUR HAND. You shall LEND to many nations, but you shall NOT BORROW. And the Lord will make you THE HEAD and not the tail, you shall be ABOVE ONLY and NOT be beneath, if you heed the commandments of the Lord your God..." (Deut. 28:8-13).

This passage describes to us the blessing of the Lord upon the works of our hands. In this prophetic hour of the final generation, these covenant promises take on a PROPHETIC CHARACTER, which means that all these promises must be fulfilled to their fullest extent in this final generation of the church. Prophetically speaking, we are the generation that will see the wonderful manifestation of all these promises in Deuteronomy 28. All the promises of God certainly belong to us in Christ Jesus, to appropriate every day. But in this final generation, all God's promises for the church become prophetic, simply because there will not be another generation of the church to fullfill any more of these unfulfilled promises in the future. No wonder Paul urges us to awake out of sleep, since our salvation is now nearer than when we first believed, even closer than what we could imagine! Romans 13:11 is therefore a prophetic word of warning for this final generation to WAKE US UP! The sleepy church needs to be shakened and awakened to the reality of these powerful forthcoming attractions! When are we going to take the plans and promises of God seriously, or are we prophetically so ignorant that we are completely insensitive to the great financial wonders of God for tomorrow?

The prophetic fulfillment of all the covenant promises of Deuteronomy 28 will elevate the church to a position of complete world domination and authority, thus enabling us to carry out the great commission of the Lord, by preaching the Gospel to every creature on earth (Mark 16:15), during the final years of this final generation!

However, the powerful grip of poverty upon the church throughout history has made Deuteronomy 28 look totally unrealistic, subsequently we have treated it nonchalantly and with unbelief. But the truth is unchangeable; this prophetic Scripture will be fulfilled in Israel during the millennium, but long before then, it will be fulfilled in the church as she launches her final invasion of salvation upon planet earth.

Let's examine the passage quoted above in Deuteronomy 28 a little closer.

THE BLESSINGS OF DOMINION

The passage in Deuteronomy 28 contains SEVEN POWERFUL COVENANT BLESSINGS OF PROSPERITY awaiting fulfillment in the end-time church. These seven blessings promised to us as an inheritance are BLESSINGS OF DOMINION. These blessings are designed to restore God's people to a full and complete dominion over the affairs of the earth. The dominion described in Deuteronomy 28 is one of AUTHORITY (governing power), one of STEWARDSHIP (possession of assets), and one of ESTABLISHMENT (to explore and develop earth's resources). This is the original dominion of Adam (Gen. 1:26-27). Of course this lost dominion of Adam was returned to us through the Lord Jesus on the cross, but the supernatural work of the Holy Spirit will practically ENFORCE the reality of this great dominion in the end-time church. Flowing out from the church, this restored dominion in all of its power will have a rippling effect throughout society and the world. By using this newfound dominion to its fullest potential, the church will then execute God's end-time plan in the earth, ruling and reigning as kings and priests, until He returns.

Let's examine these seven blessings of dominion briefly.

The FIRST BLESSING OF DOMINION is found in Deuteronomy 28:8. God says here that He will COMMAND the BLESSING on you in your STOREHOUSES. God will COMMAND it! That means the blessing will be infallible. When God commands it, it will not and cannot fail. Whatever God commands will stand forever, because it is His prophetic will. So the blessing of our storehouses will not fail. What is a storehouse? It is a place where we gather, collect and store our income, profits, and life's earnings. In the days of Israel, the harvest would be gathered from the field during the season of harvest, and then stored away in the storehouse. So the storehouse is the place where we store our profits, like the bank, investment markets, mutual funds, and the stock market. The harvest is our INCOME, AS WELL AS THE PROFITS, and performances of all our MONEY MARKET AND STOCK MARKET INVESTMENTS. People say, "But this is the world system you are talking about!" "Exactly!" Every person who earns money in this world taps into the world system. We all, some way or another, earn our respective incomes and salaries from the world system, don't we? But God has promised to bless us through the provisions of this world. The Lord says that He will COMMAND THE BLESSING upon our STOREHOUSES, and IN ALL to which you SET YOUR HAND TO! That is NATURAL labor, which pays NATURAL money out of the NATURAL world system of finances. Instead of allowing the devil's people to manipulate and control the world system as they have done for so long, God is going to bless His people with the riches of the earth. The world system with all its wealth does not belong to the devil. He has stolen it. But the earth and its fullness belong to God. Further, the wealth of THE WICKED is stored up FOR THE RIGHTEOUS!

The world system therefore, will be blessed, not cursed! NO! The sin and evil will be removed from it, and the system itself shall be turned over to God's people to correct, control, and govern. God is saying to us that He will bless the resources of the world system, so that God's people may reap the blessings of the provisions which He has placed here in the earth for the benefit of HIS servants. The people who always prosper at large through the world system are the sinners of the world, while God's people pull their noses up at money. But this is all going to change. God wants His people to be blessed through the world system, instead of the wicked people of the devil. God's intention as seen here in Deuteronomy 28 is to turn the wealth of the world over to His people, and bless them with it.

THE SECOND BLESSING OF DOMINION has to do with LOCATION. It is the promise of prosperity given to us IN THE LAND which the Lord has given us, as recorded in Deuteronomy 28:8b, which promise is again repeated to us in verse 11. It is equally important that we are in the right place for God to bestow the abundant blessings of heaven upon us. The location of operation, of course, is different for everybody. Some of us are to stay in the same location for a lifetime, yet there are others who might have to change their location several times and be transplanted in other nations by the will of the Lord. For my wife and I, this proved to be the case, and by the Word of the Lord to us, we had to leave our native South Africa to come all the way to America. The blessing of the location or country depends on this: TO BE IN THE RIGHT PLACE, AT THE RIGHT TIME, DOING THE RIGHT THING. If any of these three requirements are out of line, we cannot expect the blessing of the land to come upon us. The blessing of the land is that you will dwell safely, that you will eat the good of the land (partake of its prosperity), and that your children and descendants will be blessed also in that land after you. In order for us to be in the right place, at the right time, doing the right thing, requires for us individually to learn to listen to the voice of the Holy Spirit (see chapter 5) and go out to obey Him, once His instructions have been heard in our hearts. I believe many Christians have missed it in failing to listen to the voice of God, and have forfeited their own prosperity, because they were not in the right place, at the right time, doing the right thing.

Abraham had to migrate to a foreign land that was not known to him. But God blessed him mightily. Israel as a nation was obligated to God to return as a nation to the land of their father Abraham in a mass exodus from the land of Egypt, on a journey which was filled with great difficulty. For those of you who are Americans by birth, you need to realize that you were born in the most prosperous country in all of the modern world. If ever I have seen a land of opportunity, this is the one. However, the blessing of the land is a global blessing, not limited to any particular country only, but destined for all God's people of the last days.

THE THIRD BLESSING OF DOMINION as recorded in Deuteronomy 28:9 is the establishing of God's people as a Holy and purified people. Paul says that Jesus will return for a GLORIOUS CHURCH without spot or wrinkle. When the first miracle of this fivefold plan of blessing begins to take place, an outpouring of Holy Ghost fire will fall from heaven upon the church, purifying and refining the church almost instantly. Every born-again Christian will burn with *heavenly fire* until we are completely purified and tried by fire, presented holy and unblamable before God, while yet in our earthly vessels. The Holy Spirit's fire will simply destroy and burn up all the chaff in us, even burning up the self-nature in us upon the altar of grace. Having gone through the fire, the burnt offering of the church delivering a sweet-smelling savor in God's nostrils, would have died in Christ. We will no longer live, but Christ will live completely through us by His Holy Spirit. From here on out, the perfect will of God will be done through the church corporately, because the self-nature would be completely dead. This end-time revival, both the spiritual and the financial revival will then come forth with full acceptance of the church. The purification unto holiness would have been completed, and the body of Christ *glorified by fire* will come forth unitedly and corporately to execute the perfect will of God for this final hour.

THE FOURTH BLESSING OF DOMINION is summarized in the word EXHIBITION. In Deuteronomy 28:10, God says that He will ESTABLISH you unto Himself (in wealth), to such a great degree of riches that all the people of the earth will SEE the favour and blessing of God in your life, including the atheist. Our prosperity manifested will be supernaturally displayed to the world, so that everyone will acknowledge that it was humanly impossible to achieve; therefore it had to be the handiwork of God Himself. The blessed church of the Lord made prosperous will become God's SHOWPIECE or EXHIBITION to the world. Everyone, sinner and saint, will be able to see God's blessings upon His chosen, and the people of the world will FEAR the church because of God's miraculous blessings in our lives.

Just imagine this for a moment. The heathen will envy us, fear us, respect us, and be desperate to seek our favor. The ungodly will seek after our business, hoping that dealing with us will bring rewards for them. The commercial banks will beg for our business, and entrepreneurs, investors, and business executives will suddenly begin to fill the church pews on Sunday, hoping to receive a similar blessing from the Lord. This envious situation has already occurred in the nation of Portugal during the late eighties, when revival had caused almost 100 churches to mushroom in a matter of years, which brought about an influx of several hundred thousand new Christians into the church, including many rich business leaders. Suddenly a great deal of the wealth of that small nation shifted into the church, making it the wealthiest church in all of Europe. Financially, this newly developed situation caused an uproar in the land of Portugal. Banks and businesses were falling over their feet to earn the business of this new influential and wealthy church. This strong and ever-increasing church became the fastest growing "BUSINESS VENTURE" in the nation. The church also became a community leader in finances, and business, quickly gaining a reputation for offering the best salaries of any business firm in all of Portugal. Equipped with the most advanced technology, the church quickly set the trend for excellence. In the process of time, the computer department of the church was asked by the business community to provide training in computer technology, since they were so far advanced beyond the local business community of Lisbon. This example given of the Portugal church is only a taste of what is to come in these last days. The church will set the standard, and the world will play follow the leader!

THE FIFTH BLESSING OF DOMINION is the blessing of SUPERABUNDANCE. In Deuteronomy 28:11, the abundant overflowing blessing of God is bestowed upon us. God says that He will give us PLENTY OF GOODS (possessions); God will also bless the FRUIT OF OUR BODIES (children); He will further increase our livestock (or investments, savings, money or trade); and our produce (product, income or salary). This superabundant blessing is a mighty FOURFOLD BLESSING OF PROSPERITY. God will give us plenty of possessions, and plenty of children to help us enjoy it, and then if that's not enough, He will INCREASE our profits derived from our possessions, and give us a harvest from what we sow or give away! Let's reevaluate this amazing fourfold blessing for a moment.

1. PLENTY OF GOODS (accumulation), riches, wealth and many possessions.

2. PLENTY OF OFFSPRING (multiplication), the blessing of many children to share our possessions with.

3. INCREASE OF GOODS (acceleration), having given us plenty of goods already, now God proceeds to increase the wealth given to us.

4. THE BLESSING OF THE SOWER (harvest), the fourth thing that God promises to do for us is to give us a produce or harvest from the ground. The ground represents the place or soil where we sow our seed. The seeds that we sow will PRODUCE and yield a HARVEST. This enormous fourfold blessing is a blessing of: (1) Accumulation; (2) Multiplication; (3) Acceleration; and (4) Harvest. Glory to God! The Lord is going to release the blessing of SUPERABUNDANCE to the body of Christ.

THE SIXTH BLESSING OF DOMINION is the blessing of HEAVENLY ABUNDANCE. In Deuteronomy 28:12, God says that He will open up His HEAVENLY TREASURES to us. The original word for treasures in this verse is STOREHOUSE. God says that we can now begin to draw upon heaven's resources in addition to the earth's resources already at our disposal. This wonderful promise corresponds with the words of the prophet Malachi, who says that God will OPEN THE WINDOWS OF HEAVEN, and pour us out a blessing that we will not be able to contain (Mal. 3:10). Once again this is prophetic for our generation, since it has never been literally fulfilled, but it will happen in our final generation. Another corresponding verse with the heavenly blessing is Philippians 4:19, which says that "...my God shall supply all your need according to His RICHES IN GLORY [heaven] by Christ Jesus." The Lord will open up His heavenly storehouse for us. How do we draw upon the heavenly resources? By finding out God's will for our lives and fulfill it. By seeking the kingdom of God and gathering in lost souls into His kingdom. By doing these two things we reap a twofold blessing. God Himself will pour out an abundance of blessings that we will not be able to contain, and second, we will deposit riches in our heavenly account for us to enjoy throughout eternity. These are the treasures that Jesus told us to lay up in heaven. So, in response to our obedience, the Lord will command the heavenly blessings, treasures, and resources of the heavenly storehouse upon us!

Furthermore God will command the rain (spiritual, financial, and natural rain), upon our land. The spiritual rain of the Lord will continually fall upon us in these last days as God pours out His Spirit upon all flesh. Financially God will rain His blessing upon all our business affairs, shower after shower, giving us a new harvest every day! The rain is a symbol of God's favor and heavenly blessing for us. The rain is literally God's blessing from above. "Every good and PERFECT GIFT comes from above from the Father..." (James 1:17). The rain is God's divine favor. The last days are days of the outpouring of the rains of God, the due SEASON OF HARVEST. Besides the spiritual and financial rain, the abundance of natural rain will also be poured out upon the earth, for as it was in the days of Noah, so will it be in the days of the coming of the son of man.

But God is not done yet. He says that He will prosper us so abundantly that we will lend money to many nations, and that we will NOT BORROW. HOW MIRACULOUS!! People talk about a world bank that the antichrist will control, yet God says that His people will possess the wealth of the world and LEND TO MANY NATIONS. To me this sounds like a CHRISTIAN WORLD BANK (whether officially or unofficially I don't know). God's church of the last days will distribute the wealth of the world to all the nations, having our STOREHOUSE filled with the riches of the earth. The church will both possess the money of the earth, as well as administrate and control its distribution. Of course after the rapture of the church the antichrist will seize control of the world system, but it is not until we, the church, have ruled and reigned, subdued all things unto the name of Jesus, brought in the harvest, and is finally raptured to heaven. Therefore, *THIS HOUR BELONGS TO THE CHURCH!*

THE SEVENTH BLESSING OF DOMINION establishes the church in a position of TOTAL DOMINION. In Deuteronomy 28:13, God promises to make us the head and not the tail, and to exalt us among the peoples of the earth so that we are above only, and not beneath. This final blessing of dominion, contains a full restoration to the exact and precise dominion which Adam had had in the beginning, except that Adam's world was a perfect one. The Lord will make us the head and not the tail. As His kings and priests we will reign in this life (Rom. 5:17), through Jesus our Lord, and by the ability of the Holy Spirit in us. We will be in the driver's seat, in charge and in control of the world's affairs, first spiritually, but also financially and economically. It is this reign of the final generation of the church which the antichrist will imitate and copy, after the church is raptured. This Christ-given dominion of the last-day church will enable us to reap God's end-time harvest, and destroy all the works of the devil, including Satan's attempts through the secular world to stop the church's march upon all nations.

Let's identify the underlying theme of this prophetic word in Deuteronomy 28:

In verse 8 it is BLESSING and PROSPERITY (work of our hands).

In verse 9 it is to be ESTABLISHED (to gain authority and esteem).

In verse 10 it is to be EXALTED above all people (so greatly that people will fear you).

In verse 11 it is an ABUNDANT BLESSING (above all people).

In verse 12 it is a SUPER ABUNDANT BLESSING (with inexhaustible resources to lend to many nations).

In verse 13 it is FINANCIAL LEADERSHIP AND CONTROL OF THE RESOURCES OF EARTH.

When we combine all the highlights of this passage together they read as follows:

God will give BLESSINGS and PROSPERITY to His people, and ESTABLISH them financially, so that they become EXALTED in the earth, favored above all people, and PROSPERED so SUPER ABUNDANTLY with the wealth of the earth, that they may assume a complete FINANCIAL LEADERSHIP OF THE EARTH, WITH FULL CONTROL OF ALL ITS RESOURCES.

GOVERNMENT

Isaiah said of Jesus that the GOVERNMENT shall rest upon His shoulders (Isa. 9:6). We are the body of Christ. Our head is in heaven. But the shoulders are a part of the body on earth, not a part of the head in heaven. So, even as far back as Isaiah, it was prophesied that the church will rule and reign and subdue all things, having had Christ put ALL THINGS UNDER OUR FEET (Eph. 1:22-23). Our headship will be total and complete. We will be the head and not the tail. Right now the church is the tail in everything, but thank God, it is fixing to change drastically. Armed with the vision of fulfilling the great commission, the church will reign financially by distributing the wealth of the world as needed, and reap the world harvest for the Lord's return.

Let's conclude this chapter with a consideration of some scriptural examples of the blessing of the Lord upon the work of our hands.

(Genesis 26) You are probably familiar with the miraculous situation that occurred in Isaac's life when the Lord told him to sow seed during the time of a severe famine as he dwelt in the land of Gerar. Yet by the Word of the Lord, Isaac sowed in the drought-stricken soil of Gerar and reaped in the SAME YEAR A HUNDREDFOLD RETURN, and the Lord blessed him. This was not all, though. The Lord continued to prosper him until Isaac became VERY prosperous. Eventually Isaac's wealth was so great that he took away the prosperity of the Philistines in their own land and they began to envy him. The situation was so threatening to King Abimelech, that he finally told Isaac to move away from their land. But the blessing of the Lord upon Isaac was unmistakable. Naturally speaking, he had no chance of becoming rich. He lived among strangers, and the country was experiencing a severe famine. But God supernaturally and MIRACULOUSLY blessed the work of his hands, and Isaac prospered against all odds.

JACOB: THE SPECKLED AND SPOTTED SPECTACLE

(Genesis 30) When Laban realized that God was blessing him because of his nephew Jacob, he convinced Jacob to stay with him and remain in his service. When Laban offered Jacob a wage, Jacob said that he wanted nothing. His only request was to remove the speckled and spotted sheep and goats (usually the weaker and inferior ones) from Laban's flocks for himself. By starting out with the "leftovers" of his uncle's flocks, Jacob's chances of prospering naturally were almost none. But the miraculous intervention of God turned all that around. God prospered the flocks of Jacob and multiplied them numerously. The weaker speckled and spotted flocks became the stronger and healthier flocks, leaving Laban's flocks feebler. Once again the underdog was king of the castle, because God had prospered Jacob supernaturally. The turnaround of events was so spectacular that Laban became extremely jealous of Jacob until finally Jacob was forced to take all his wealth and family, and flee to Canaan. Unusual situations like these ones are just perfect for God to intervene upon and turnaround for His people in these last days.

JOSEPH: FROM THE PIT TO THE KING'S PALACE

(Genesis 39-45) The phenomenal story of Joseph's rise to stardom is another example of how God can supernaturally bless the works of our hands. Delivered into a dark pit in the ground by his jealous brothers, and doomed to a life of slavery in Egypt, Joseph's chances of becoming prosperous were almost impossible. But when God supernaturally intervened, Joseph was propelled to the second highest office in the land of Egypt. For the next seven years following Joseph's sudden rise to prominence, the hands of this former slave were blessed with prosperity like never before. Under his leadership, Joseph administered the greatest storage operation of food in the history of the ancient empires. When the prophesied famine began to take effect after the seven-year period of prosperity had ended, Joseph fulfilled the Scriptures by "lending to many nations and having no need to borrow at all." Joseph became the bread basket of the world, feeding the nations with the abundance of food in Egypt. Joseph went from the pit to prison, to the deputy ruler of Egypt, to becoming the provider of the nations, and being the overseer of the storehouse of the world. The blessing of the Lord fell upon the hands of Joseph.

Joseph is a prophetic example of the final generation of the church. The final seven-year period of the church on earth before the rapture will place the church in a "Joseph situation," feeding the entire world with food, both spiritual as well as natural. The spiritual food that the church will provide will be the fulfillment of the great commission, in preaching the Gospel to literally EVERY CREATURE, in order to reap the final harvest. The bread of life will flow out from the church to the nations. After inheriting the wealth of the wicked, the church will also feed the nations with natural food, which will gather the nations together at the feet of the church, just like all people from all nations came from afar to purchase food from Joseph. At the end of this glorious seven-year period of feeding the nations both spiritually and naturally, the church will be raptured. Immediately after the rapture of the church, the seven years of famine as described in the Book of Revelation will commence. The rider on the black horse will announce the most severe famine ever to curse the earth (Rev. 6:5-6). This second seven-year period resembling the times of Joseph will be the seven-year tribulation period, a time of terrible famine. So this prophetic 14-year period in the life of Joseph is an exact prophetic type and forerunner of the final 14-year period before the end of the age. The seven years of famine (tribulation) will conclude with the return of Christ, Israel's deliverance, and the commencement of the 1000-year millennium of peace. But the first seven years will be glorious for the church to fulfill. Under a "Joseph's anointing," we will feed the world, spiritually and physically.

DANIEL: FROM CAPTIVITY TO CAPTAIN

(Daniel 2) Daniel was taken captive by King Nebuchadnezzar as a prisoner in Babylon. While in custody, his light began to shine. God prospered him physically, and when the king was troubled and his sleep left him by some mysterious dreams, the blessing of God upon Daniel enabled him to recall the dream and explain its interpretation. Instantly Daniel was promoted to chief administrator of Babylon, from a prisoner to a prince in one day. The blessing of the Lord supernaturally thrust Daniel into a lifetime position of authority and prosperity, which was a miraculous wonder of God.

PROPHETIC HOUR

Each of the above mentioned examples took place during very crucial prophetic times in the plans of God for the future. Today (1996), the church lives in an absolute pivotal period of prophetic time, as the end of the dispensation of grace draws to a close. Let us begin to anticipate the fulfillment of some great prophetic wonders in this final hour of the church, and the miraculous exploits of God that are about to burst upon the scene, repeating and surpassing the blessings of God of old.

Here are some of the most prevalent blessings of the Lord for us to anticipate in the near future:

1. The blessing of the Lord upon the works of our hands (Deut. 12:18, 16:15, 24:19, Job 1:10, Ps. 90:17).

2. The blessing of sowing in famine (Gen. 26).

3. The blessing of supernatural favour and promotions (Joseph) (Gen. 41).

4. The blessing of the hundredfold return (Isaac) (Gen. 26:12, Matt. 13:8-23, 19:29, Mark 10:30, Luke 8:8).

5. The blessing of investments (parable of the talents) (Matt. 25:20).

6. The blessing of the sower (Matt. 13:3, 18, Mark 4:3, 14, Luke 8:5, 2 Cor. 8).

7. The blessing of the ministry, or the New Testament priesthood (1 Cor. 9:9-14).

8. The blessing of the soul winner (Matt. 6:33).

9. The blessing of the tither (Mal. 3:10).

10. The blessing of the business entrepreneur, or merchant (Matt. 13:44, 47-48, Matt. 20:1-16).

The blessings of Deuteronomy 28 substantiates everyone of the ten above mentioned blessings of the works of our hands. These ten blessings avail themselves for God to use in these last days to SUPERNATURALLY increase the body of Christ and bless us in our professions, respectively. The rise of the church in the place of business and finances will be the FIRST STEP in God's plan to elevate the church to a position of total dominance in the world during these last days. When we begin to see the favour of the Lord establishing Christians as leaders in the business community, we need to prepare for a second financial miracle to follow shorty after. This second miracle is THE TRANSFERENCE OF THE WEALTH OF THE SINNER TO THE RIGHTEOUS. At this time, the world is REALLY going to be shaken, because her wealth will suddenly change hands from the wicked to the righteous children of God. The first event of God's financial plan is a mere blessing of our income. The second event will add the INCOME (wealth), of the world to our possessions. At this point and time, the revival takes on a new dimension. The church is not only "EARNING" good money. NO! At this given point and time, we also "INHERIT" the wealth of the entire world system on top of our profits.The wealth of the wicked is now placed in the hands of God's people! Wealth is simply flowing into the church in great proportions!

3 | The Wealth of the Wicked

"...the wealth of the sinner is stored up for the righteous." Proverbs 13:22, NKJV

The planet earth and its environment was originally created for mankind and his subordinates. Following his immediate creation, the first man called Adam was given a universal authority over the entire earth. This God-given authority was a complete and total authority over all the earth, including every living thing upon the planet and in the sea. Adam subsequently received the power of "DOMINION." The concept of dominion can best be described as a God-given ability to be LORD over something; to RULE and REIGN; to have divinely delegated authority as well as decision-making power invested in you; or to possess an appointed KINGSHIP or LORDSHIP over things.

God entrusted the power of dominion to Adam (Gen. 1:26). Adam became no less than a little "god" of the planet, a lord, with all the governing powers and decision-making abilities regarding the earth placed at his disposal. Adam's dominion was a pure and perfectly autonomous, self-ruled authority. This same Adamic authority was restored to mankind by the Lord Jesus when He was raised from the dead. Prior to His departure to heaven, the Lord reinstated this authority to His followers by saying, "All authority has been given to Me in heaven and on earth. Go therefore..." (Matt. 28:18). The lordship of Adam lost through sin was restored to mankind ONLY through the salvation of Jesus Christ and partaken of ONLY through the new birth of the human spirit unto an eternal redemption. We learn from this fact that God's plan with man has always been the same in essence which is to make him a creature of "DOMINION." God made Adam a king, and committed a kingdom into his trust. Let's consider this:

1. Adam was created a king with the power of dominion. He reigned until he fell into sin.

2. Jesus has restored kingship to us through His gift of salvation. We can now reign IN THIS LIFE in Christ Jesus as kings (Rom. 5:17).

3. During the 1000-year reign of the Messiah, we, the church, WILL REIGN with Christ on the earth (Rev. 20:4).

4. After the final judgement, God's people WILL REIGN with Christ over His eternal kingdom (Rev. 2:26-27).

OWNERSHIP AND STEWARDSHIP

Some people teach that God gave Adam the title deed or proof of OWNERSHIP of the planet, when He appointed Adam as king of the earth. However, that is not true. Adam received STEWARDSHIP of the earth and not "OWNERSHIP." If Adam had in fact received total ownership of the earth, God could never have found a way to return to earth Himself in order to redeem us again after Adam's fall. Satan simply would not have allowed that to happen.

In explaining man's position of stewardship in the earth, Jesus said on occasion that the kingdom of God is like a "LANDOWNER" (Jesus) who went out early in the morning to HIRE laborers (people) for his vineyard (Matt. 20:1). The Lord is the landowner of earth, and people the laborers sent by the Lord to work in God's fields. Jesus told His disciples that He is the Lord of the harvest, and that He is looking for laborers to go out to reap His harvest (Matt. 9:36-38). Jesus also told the story of the kingdom of God being like a man (Jesus) traveling to a far country, who called His servants and delivered HIS GOODS to them (Matt. 25:14).

The man (Jesus), delivered different amounts of talents to each of His servants before His departure. After His subsequent return, He required an account given of each of the servants separately. However, the servant who received only one talent did not gain any more talents. To him the Lord said as follows: "...you ought to have deposited MY MONEY with the bankers, and at my coming I would have received back MY OWN with interest" (Matt. 25:27). According to the parable, the Lord required an account given of His possessions entrusted to His servants. Even during His absence, the Lord was still the sole possessor of the gifts and talents given to His servants. The servants became the "STEWARDS" of the Master's goods, accountable to the Master for the use of those goods at the Master's return.

The fact of the matter is that God always remains the CREATOR, OWNER and POSSESSOR of the entire creation on earth, its substances, all its living creatures, including all the gifts, talents and abilities entrusted to them. But, with Adam's fall, Satan became the new "STEWARD" of our planet. So the devil became the manager and administrator of God's planet. He became the god of the world system, but not the planet itself.

Let's use the story of a store and its store owner to illustrate this fact: When Adam fell into sin, he lost his stewardship (position of manager to the store) including his authority and dominion to the devil. Satan then became the steward of earth (manager of the store) but he did not become the owner of the store. God is the sole owner of the store (earth), which is not for sale! Satan's new position gave him the control of, and administrative power over the earth. He had become the "god" of the world system, able to control and manipulate all of the earth's affairs. Through partnership with man, however, the door would always be open for God to send His Son into the earth as a man, to reverse the perversion of the earth's authority. Satan, however, is so ridiculous. When Jesus came to the earth, he took Him up on a high mountain, showed Him all the kingdoms of the earth, and told Jesus emphatically that all these things had been given to him. That was only a half-truth. But then again the devil is such a liar, manipulator and thief, that he would naturally try very hard to deceive the Lord Jesus concerning the issue of the stewardship of the earth. In his desperation to retain the stolen stewardship of Adam, the devil offered Jesus a flaky "BUSINESS DEAL." Here is the devil's pack of lies presented to the Lord:

First, Satan offered Jesus ownership of earth, when the earth was not his to give away, since it is already Christ's possession. (The devil tries to sell Jesus the store, yet Jesus is already the owner of the store).

Second, the devil offers Jesus the possessions and wealth of the earth (or the merchandise of the store), when the possessions of the earth or the goods of the store are not his to sell. The fullness or wealth of the earth already belonged to the Lord. Let's combine points one and two together in this Scripture."The earth and its fullness are the Lord's..." (Ps. 50:12). First, the earth is the Lord's and second, the earth's fullness (or all the merchandise of the store), are also the Lord's possessions. Both the earth and all its substances have remained the Lord's possessions and are not for sale, nor can the devil offer them for sale to the Lord, since they are not his possessions to sell.

Third, the devil offered Jesus the stewardship of the earth (or the managerial position of the store). This third and final item offered here was the only thing which the devil could legally trade, since Adam was the one who turned this stewardship over to him. So of the three things which the devil tried to sell to Jesus, the stewardship of the earth was the only commodity which Satan could trade, since he had jurisdiction over the earth since the fall of Adam. But Jesus was no fool. He needed to regain control of the management of the earth again, but was not about to sell His soul to the devil. Satan believed that Jesus was vulnerable to his illegitimate offer because of His love for people and His desire to redeem them. But instead of playing games with the devil, the Lord had His own plan of action ready to be set in motion. Even though Jesus' own plan would cost Him His life, it would succeed in the end, and would ultimately prove to be a far greater plan than the devil's illegitimate offer.

Here is Jesus' ingenious plan, brilliantly devised in heaven long before the foundation of the earth:

Being sent by the Father to earth, Jesus was now present in the store (earth). He soon found the devil's escape route to his secretive underground office (hell), where he was directing all his evil operations of the store (earth). Jesus quickly slipped down the fire escape that led into the devil's underground office (hell), and caught him by surprise, while he was sleeping behind his desk. Jesus immediately opened up the devil's books, and began to examine his operations and office procedures personally. By doing this Jesus soon exposed the devil's illegal operations, fraud, evil schemes and unlawful management of the earth and its affairs. Having exposed the devil's illegal dark dealings, Jesus gave him a rude awakening, and fired him on the spot, based on professional misconduct. Jesus knew that after exposing the devil and terminating him as earth's manager, that the devil would challenge Him to a dual, and put up the fight of his life. But Jesus was ready for him. Even though all the devil's store employees (demons), rushed to his aid, fighting alongside the devil against Jesus, the wildest office brawl in the history of the universe would see Jesus triumph as the clear and undisputed winner. He simply wiped out both the devil and all his demons in open warfare, triumphing over them in hell (office). After that, Jesus simply reached into the devil's desk, picked up the office keys (the keys of death, hell and the grave) (Rev. 1:18), as well as all the keys of the store (the keys of the kingdom) (Matt. 16:19), and put them in his pocket. But before He left hell, He destroyed the devil's office. Walking back into the store (earth), Jesus handed over all the store keys (keys of the kingdom), to His beloved friends and followers. But the devil's office keys (keys of death, hell and the grave), He kept to Himself. Subsequently, Jesus promptly appointed His followers to run the store for Him, with the store keys he had just given them (keys of the kingdom of earth). Jesus also related to His friends everything that had transpired in the devil's office, and that Satan and his demons were all dismissed for professional misconduct, so noted by the high court of heaven. Subsequently, the devil and all his employees, the demons, would not be eligible for unemployment claims. The worker's union (heaven's host), would also deny the devil's protest and demands for reinstatement as the manager of the earth. The devil was simply stripped of all authority and power, and legal rights previously possessed upon the earth. What an awesome victory Jesus had won, and what a Glorious plan God had conceived before the foundation of the earth! Jesus bought back Adam's stewardship from Satan in an absolute ingenious way, and paid the full price for it through death, hell and the grave, until the Father of heaven determined that it was completely done. Praise God!

MELCHIZEDEK

Let's talk about Melchizedek, who was the pre-incarnate Christ. When Melchizedek appeared to Abram, he declared to him that God is the possessor of heaven and earth. And, of course, this incident took place after the fall of Adam. So Adam's stewardship of earth was already lost to the devil, yet Melchizedek reminds Abram of the fact that God is still the possessor of heaven as well as earth (Gen.14:18), in spite of Adam's fall into sin. If God had entrusted the ownership of the earth to Adam which was subsequently lost to the devil through Adam's fall as some scholars teach, Melchizedek's words would have been a lie. But thank God they were true. Furthermore, if Adam had lost God's entrusted ownership of the earth to the devil, it would have been impossible for God to reenter the earth after Adam's fall, furthermore it would have been equally impossible for God to make a new covenant agreement with any man upon the earth after Adam's fall and subsequent loss of the ownership of the earth. But we read in Psalm 50:12 that God says, "If I were hungry, I would not tell you; For the world is MINE, and all its fullness." Once again, this was stated long before Jesus died on the cross to redeem us. The earth has always belonged to God, who gave Adam "STEWARDSHIP" over the earth, and gave him the power of "DOMINION" to carry out that stewardship on His behalf.

RENEWED STEWARDSHIP

Adam became the king of the earth, and partook of his stewardship by being created. His stewardship was one of "CREATION." Through Jesus, every child of God receives a stewardship of "SALVATION" when we are born again. Adam got his stewardship through CREATION, we receive ours through RECREATION. But this is not all. The stewardship of salvation has much more to offer the believer in Christ. Everything that God's hands touch to restore is usually restored in a DOUBLE PORTION BLESSING. When God finally refurbished the earth after the former rebellion of Lucifer, He made it twice as beautiful, and created man twice as beautiful as Lucifer was originally created.

The same is true concerning the future. The outpouring of the Spirit in these last days will be a double portion outpouring before the Lord's return (James 5:7). During the 1000-year millennial reign of Christ succeeding the great tribulation, Israel will be restored as a nation to double glory. The new heavens and earth will be twice as beautiful as the earth was in the beginning days of Adam. The same principle is true regarding the restoration of Adam's lost stewardship through the Lord Jesus. When Jesus ascended into heaven He sat down at the right hand of the Father, where we are now seated "IN HIM" (Eph. 2:5-6). Being in Christ at the right hand of the Father, we are now blessed with "ALL SPIRITUAL BLESSINGS" so that God will supply all our needs according to His "RICHES IN GLORY." Therefore, the restoration of Adam's lost stewardship includes the restoration of both the original earthly stewardship, as well as an additional stewardship being added called "THE HEAVENLY STEWARDSHIP." Being joint heirs of Christ gives us access to all spiritual blessings in Christ in heaven, enabling God to supply our needs based not only upon earth's riches, but also by His heavenly riches in glory. The devil thought that he was very smart when he successfully stole Adam's earthly stewardship from him. But now Satan will live forever to regret this violation, because Jesus came to earth, not only to restore Adam's stolen stewardship. NO! He went one step further, He includes and also provides the stewardship of heaven as an additional blessing, a "BONUS." HALLELUJAH!

This dualistic stewardship of the new covenant also includes all the blessings of both the old and the new covenant. When Jesus died on the cross, He removed all the curses of the old covenant for us, and added all the blessings of the old covenant to us (called the blessings of Abraham) (Gal. 3:13-14). So the blessings of the new covenant in fact include all the blessings of both covenants supported by a dualistic stewardship, namely, the stewardship of the earth and the stewardship of heaven. Double stewardship and double covenant blessings! It seems as if God is absolutely adamant about His intention to prosper us, and that He would do everything possible to ensure that. God has therefore blessed us with "QUADRUPLE PROSPERITY." Double stewardship and double covenant blessings. GOD WANTS US TO PROSPER!

END-TIME MIRACLE

Prior to the church's departure to heaven, the full substance of the earth will be transferred to the church, thus fulfilling the prophetic predictions of God's Word concerning the wealth of the church in the last days. As in the days of old, the spoils of the enemies of God (the sinners, heathen), will be taken back by the people of God. The wealth of the wicked laid up for the righteous will be shifted to the people of God. Prophetically, this prediction has taken place on several occasions in the past, as recorded in God's Word. Here are a few examples from the Scriptures concerning the transfer of the wealth of the wicked to the righteous in Bible times. These examples are prophetic forerunners of a similar fulfillment of the Scriptures in the very near future. But in these last days there will be a mighty explosion of wealth that will flood the church overnight. The latter shall always be greater than the former! Let us consider the following thrilling examples from God's Word:

ISRAEL: DEPARTING EGYPT FOR THE PROMISED LAND

The ancient biblical exodus of Israel out of the land of Egypt is a prophetic replica or forerunner of the last days of the church. The ungodly Egyptian empire which was the kingdom of wealth at the time, represents the sinner or ungodly people of the last days, prior to the church's departure to heaven. Israel represents the church, the people of God. Pharaoh, king of Egypt, represents Satan in his defiance of God. Canaan, or the promised land, represents heaven, the glorious destiny of the church. The exodus itself represents the catching away or rapture of the church. Shortly before her departure from Egypt, Israel was delivered from the oppression of Pharaoh and the Egyptians through a series of supernatural and notable miracles. These supernatural exploits of God broke every bondage that Egypt had gained over Israel. Once Israel was totally delivered from the oppression of Egypt's rule, the time had arrived for departure. Supernaturally empowered by God's Spirit, Israel now plunders the land, taking possession of all things, including cattle, livestock and every living thing, as well as their gold, silver and clothing. The Egyptians gave up their possessions WILL-

INGLY. THE WEALTH OF THE SINNER WAS STORED UP FOR THE RIGHTEOUS!

This glorious prophetic incident will play itself out again before the church departs from the earth to heaven. As the church, we will experience the same phenomenon. The power of God will deliver the church supernaturally from the hold of "Pharaoh" (the devil) and the Egyptians (the world system), giving us complete command of power over our enemies. With Satan and all our enemies securely under our feet, the wealth of the world will be turned over to the church in an instant. In witnessing the reality of the same miracle being performed, the church will use the newfound wealth to gather in the "spoils" of lost souls, to take with us to the heavenly promised land when we depart the earth in a glorious "exodus" called the "rapture."

ABRAHAM AND ISRAEL

Abraham, for instance, seized the possessions of the kings after defeating them in war. On their way to the promised land, Israel overcame many enemy nations in warfare, enabling her to seize the possessions and wealth of their defeated foes. Throughout her years of occupation in the promised land, Israel would defeat numerous surrounding nations in battle. Such conflicts allowed Israel to carry away all the wealth (spoils) of her enemies. The same prophetic scenario will play itself out again between Israel and her enemies in the near future. Even before the rapture of the church takes place, Israel will again seize all her lost territories in the Middle East and will take away the possessions of her Arab neighbours through warfare. This newfound wealth will enable Israel to be restored as one of the wealthiest nations of earth, even before the departure of the church. Enabled by wealth, Israel will resettle all her people, including the returning Jews from around the world, and rebuild the economy of the nation as well as all the sacred places of worship, including the historical rebuilding of the temple in Jerusalem. This newfound wealth and sudden bloom of Israel will make her most vulnerable for attack from Russia, which will result in World War III (see Ezek. 38 and 39). Being devastated by the antichrist during the seven years of tribulation, Zechariah 14:14 informs us assuredly that all the wealth of the nations will once again be returned to Israel after the battle of Armageddon has taken place at the end of the tribulation, when Jesus returns from heaven to deliver His people from their oppressor.

The hour of glory for the church, however, is much closer than for Israel. The restoration of the wealth of the wicked to the church will take place in the very near future. Presently, discouraged through doubt, unbelief and scepticism, many Christians have sadly lost sight of God's vision for the last days. These discouraged brethren are prevented by their circumstances from aspiring to these great forthcoming prophetic miracles of wealth. Yet God will raise up His people out of the ashes of despair and pour His Spirit and glorious fire into His body worldwide. Rejuvenated, refreshed and revived by God's power, the church will suddenly spring to life and to task, first watching God perform the restorative miracle of finances, and then launch out into the deep waters of lost humanity to bring in the greatest catch of fish ever, THE FINAL HARVEST.

The following biblical example is probably the most extraordinary prophetic forerunner of the return of the wicked's wealth to the righteous. This next story shows us how God will accomplish the miraculous transfer of wealth into the church of the last days in only "ONE DAY."

During the days of the prophet Elisha, the king of Syria, on occasion gathered his army together and besieged Samaria. Already in a state of famine, the situation soon grew worse throughout Samaria. The result was one of the most severe famines in the history of Israel. A donkey's head was sold for 80 shekels (equivalent of approximately 80 U.S. dollars today, a vast sum of money in those days). The situation worsened. One day the king of Israel encountered a woman who related a horrific story to him how she had killed her son the day before and actually prepared his flesh for a meal between herself and her friend. The next day, however, the woman's friend broke her deal of the bargain by hiding her son away so that he could not be slaughtered in the same fashion. Hearing this shocking story, the king rent his clothes, and immediately sent out a messenger to the house of Elisha the prophet to kill him. (Elisha was blamed for the terrific famine in Samaria). But Elisha responded to this threat by prophesying an unbelievable word of prophecy. He said, "Tomorrow about this time a measure of fine flour shall be sold for a shekel (one U.S dollar), and two measures of barley will also be sold for a shekel, at the gate of Samaria." Bear in mind now that a donkey's head was sold for 80 shekels, yet suddenly the next day the famine is supposed to be over, dropping the price of precious merchandise to a dollar a piece. That was impossible! The fields were dry. Even if it rains for 24 hours nonstop, it will take an entire season to plant the grain and reap the crops at the end of the season. THIS IS IMPOSSIBLE! One of the officers of the king standing by said, "Look, if the Lord would make windows in heaven, could this thing be?" And the prophet of God said, "In fact, you shall see it with your eyes, but you shall not eat of it" (2 Kings 7:1-2).

What an absolute impossible prophecy! The prophet of God has surely become a liar. At that same time four leprous men sat at the city gate, contemplating their fate. If they go into the city they will die of famine, if they remain there they will die anyway. So they decided to surrender themselves to the Syrians and be kept alive with food or be killed anyway. At twilight they rose to go to the camp of the Syrians to surrender themselves to the enemy. But to their utmost surprise, there was not a single soul present in the camp of the Syrians. All of them had seemingly vanished. The lepers were unaware of the fact that the Lord had caused a great noise of chariots and many horses to be heard in the camp of the Syrians. Frightened by the seeming approach of some great army, the Syrians fled their camp hastily and in terror, leaving everything behind, completely intact. The Syrian camp was filled with an abundance of food and drink, livestock, horses, donkeys, silver, gold, plenty of clothing, precious commodities of great wealth, and all sorts of precious merchandise in an abundant supply. As soon as the four lepers overcame the initial element of shock and surprise, they decided to hurry back to Israel to reveal their wonderful discovery to the king. In hearing their unbelievable story, the king of Samaria decided to send an envoy of soldiers over to the camp of the Syrians to investigate the claims of the lepers, though fearful that this situation was an ambush set up for him by the Syrians. As the king's men began to track the path of the Syrians from the camp, they found that the road was filled with garments and weapons which the Syrians had thrown down in their haste to get away. The messengers returned with joy to confirm the story of the lepers to the king. Then the people of Israel went out to plunder the camp of the Syrians, taking all the spoils of the enemy for themselves. And literally overnight there was an abundance of food and wealth in Israel according to the Word of the Lord. A measure of flour was sold for a shekel and two measures of barley for a shekel. Then the officer who objected to the prophet of God speaking the prophecy, was trampled under foot in the city gate as the people desperately thronged together to obtain some food.

In one day, the nation of Israel at the brink of total starvation due to this severe famine, was rescued supernaturally. God simply caused all the Syrians to flee their camp in haste, leaving behind everything for God's people to possess. The wealth of the wicked was simply turned over to Israel in a single day.

24-HOUR PROSPERITY FOR THE CHURCH

Let's connect this prophetically miraculous event to the end-time church.

At present the church worldwide is in an impoverished state, suffering from lack in every area. Some of the hierarchy of the church blame God's prophets for the famine. They are being called "FLAKY" and "AB-SURD" in their prophecies of God's plan for these last days. But the prophets of God will respond to the accusations with a profound prophetic word straight from the mouth of God. When the word of prophecy is made known, a spirit of unbelief will manifest itself among the religious leadership of the church, scoffing at the prophets of God, and rejecting God's Word of an instantaneous miracle of prosperity. They will say that even if God makes windows in the heavens, this miracle would be impossible. Through a series of supernatural visions God will convince the sinners controlling the world system to recklessly abandon all their possessions, and run. Through fear of a sudden market crash, forecasted by all financiers and investment experts, unbelievers will simply give away their stocks and investments. Being led by the Spirit of God, the Church community, however, would take up the abandoned stocks and occupy the entire market share, which soon would turn to gold.

We can only speculate as to how God will ingeniously perform such a miracle. But the prophetic truth remains unshakable. The wealth of the wicked shall be given to the righteous. It will be ours for the taking. After the great shake-up the world will begin to fear and respect the church for the first time. Stunned by the sudden change of events, the wicked will begin to pour into the church and get saved, as well as invest whatever money they have left in the church. This will be an outstanding wonder of modern times. And it will happen overnight, within a 24-hour period of time. Suddenly, the wealth of the sinners will become the property of the righteous, but woe to the religious leaders who mocked God's Word saying it was a fantasy, they will be judged by God, and die the very same day. They will not partake of the newfound wealth of the church nor will they live to enjoy the subsequent end-time revival triggered by this phenomenal miracle.

Some people will say that this is a ridiculous analogy, yet the Word of God supports miraculous events like this one for the last days of the church on earth. Be prepared and ready, dear Christian, because your eyes will see the glory of the Lord in these days. Be on the lookout for the spirit of unbelief and skepticism which is working among our ranks in the church. This pessimistic, skeptical spirit will cause people to call this kind of prediction "RIDICULOUS, FARFETCHED, IMPOSSIBLE AND ABSURD." Allow your spirit to be filled with faith, expectation, and excitement for the great miracles of God in these last days, which are now just around the corner. Move on into the anointing of the Holy Spirit and the flow of His power because the end-time miracles of God can only be aspired to when we walk in the supernatural flow of God's Spirit, and not in the foolishness of our own minds. You will then both see and experience this great blessing that awaits us, otherwise you will become like the unbelieving generation of Israel in the wilderness, and will pass on to glory not able to live out these glorious days of revival on the earth. (Just like Israel, on the way to the promised land.) Those who draw back because of unbelief in this final hour will not enter in with us, but will fall by the wayside. Death will come to the unbelieving just like the king's servant who died, looking at the manifestation of the miracle, yet was not able to enjoy the fruit thereof. Be ready and be prepared, for the Lord is coming soon, but be on the lookout because the great miracles come first, starting with the financial transformation of the monetary systems of the world.

In the words of the prophet Isaiah we announce to the church: "Arise, shine, For your light has come! And the glory of the Lord is risen upon you. The Gentiles [sinners] shall come to your light, And kings to the BRIGHTNESS OF YOUR RISING. Because the ABUNDANCE of the sea [people] shall be turned to you, THE WEALTH OF THE GENTILES SHALL COME TO YOU [wealth of the wicked]. And I will glorify the house of My glory" (Isaiah 60:1,3,5b and 7c). THIS IS WHAT WILL BE FULFILLED PROPHETICALLY IN THE CHURCH! It is time for the church to wake up prophetically, to this hour of the glory of the Lord which is upon us. It is time to arise and shine, because God has given us the heathen, even the nations of the earth, as our INHERITANCE!

4 | *The Gold and the Glory*

> *"...I will fill this temple with glory, says the Lord of hosts. The silver is Mine, and the gold is Mine, says the Lord of hosts."* Haggai 2:7-8, NKJV

The revelation of the gold and the glory came to me on Tuesday, August 17, 1993, at approximately 12 noon. I was preaching in a church in a small town called Spindale in North Carolina. Even though revelation of God's Word comes to us as a progressive thing, a revelation imparted by the Spirit of God usually comes instantaneously. It happened suddenly, while I was teaching during a morning service. I saw something like a bright light flash before my eyes. This incident might sound quite spectacular as I am relating the story here, but the light passed before me so quickly, that all I could do was to blink my eyes briefly, paused momentarily, and found myself rather startled and not at all sure as to what had happened. I tried to resume my message, but found myself rather disoriented at the time. In the minutes that followed, while recovering from the "DISTURBANCE" that had happened only seconds before, I felt something soft and very pleasant rise up within me, filling first my throat and then my mouth. It was at this point that I opened my mouth spontaneously, to allow the new flood of words welling up within me to escape audibly. It took almost two hours to empty my mouth of all the wonderful words which the Holy Spirit had filled my spirit with so surprisingly. As a result of this inspired utterance, a new message was birthed which I quickly entitled "THE GOLD AND THE GLORY." Since receiving this message from the Lord that day, my life and ministry have both been totally revolutionized by its phenomenal truth. This message brought about a turnaround in my approach to biblical finances and has subsequently yielded the fruit of financial blessing in our ministry. The message of the gold and the glory was given to me by the Lord concerning God's end-time plan of a financial revival for the church.

Both the message of the gold and the glory, and the idea of writing this book, were conceived in my spirit during that unforgettable morning service. I personally know of other ministers who have carried this message from our ministry to theirs, who can now testify of an increase in their finances. The same is true for many Christians who have received this message through the preaching of God's Word. In a relatively short time, numerous testimonies have been verified concerning this message. "THE GOLD AND THE GLORY" is a prophetic message for the end-time church, and is part and parcel of God's end-time financial revival for the church. I trust that you will fall in love with the story of the Gold and the Glory, just as I did, but also that you will be inspired to pursue the "GLORY" of God, in order to receive the blessing of the "GOLD," in your life. The gold and the glory of God is coming back to the house of God in these last days.

The prophetic message of the *Gold and the Glory* was delivered through the mouth of the prophet Haggai as follows:

"For thus says the Lord of hosts: 'Once more (it is a little while) I will shake heaven and earth, the sea and dry land; and I will shake all nations, and they shall come to the Desire of All Nations, and I will fill this temple with GLORY,' says the Lord of hosts. 'The silver is Mine, and the GOLD is Mine,' says the Lord of hosts. 'The GLORY of this latter temple shall be greater than the former,' says the Lord of hosts. 'And in this place I will give peace,' says the Lord of hosts" (Hag. 2:6-9).

Let me say, first of all, that I am aware of the dualistic application of this particular passage of Scripture. Its reference is made first in the interest of the nation of Israel. The context clearly shows that. The Lord is instructing Haggai to address Zerubbabel the governor of Judah with this word. Zerubbabel stands at the head of the returning exiles' effort to rebuild the old temple of Solomon. Since Nebuchadnezzar's invasion of Jerusalem in the year 606 B.C., the temple after being plundered and vandalized had remained in ruins for a period of 150 years or three jubilees. Opposition to the rebuilding of the temple soon came from local adversaries in the land as they contended with the Israelites over their desired participation in the work on the new temple.

They sent a letter to King Artaxerxes objecting to the new project, and managed to sway the king to their persuasion. Subsequently, the command is given to abort the work, and the new decree and its command was enforced upon Israel by her enemies. In Ezra 5 we read the account of the prophets Haggai and Zechariah, as they begin to prophesy to the Jews, telling them by the Word of the Lord that they should resume the work on the temple. In obedience to the prophetic words received, the Jews immediately took up the strenuous task again, but Israel's enemies retaliated by drafting another letter of objection; this time addressing it to King Darius. After careful consideration was given to the matter, the king issued a decree that the temple should in fact be reconstructed. The prophecy recorded in chapter 2 was given by Haggai to Zerubbabel to encourage him to resume the work on the Temple (Hag. 2:6-9).

This prophecy was the first historical account given to Zerubbabel. Subsequently, the work on the temple was resumed, and finally completed according to the prophetic words which were given through the prophets Haggai and Zachariah. So the second temple of Israel was built to completion as a result of this prophecy. But in these last days Israel will once again act upon the prophetic words of these two prophets, by rebuilding the temple yet one more time. Just as the prophecies regarding the rebuilding of the temple resulted in the reconstruction of the second temple of old, so the same prophecies will once again inspire Israel to rebuild their third and final temple, and complete the task even before the rapture of the church.

But there is also a subsequent or secondary application of this prophecy which effects the modern-day church of the Lord Jesus Christ. The creative power of this profound prophecy is going to have a resounding effect and impact upon the end-time church, drastically altering her destiny.

THE CHURCH OF GOLD AND GLORY

During the times of the old covenant, Israel as the children of the promise to Abraham were the house of God, or God's covenant people. The Abrahamic Covenant and all its futuristic promises did not become obsolete since the new covenant of Christ was consummated on Calvary. Rather, the promises of God to Israel are only to be delayed for a time, they will be fulfilled during the great millennial of peace after the Messiah's return for Israel and their great deliverance at the battle of Armageddon. Salvation is for the Jew first, but also for the Gentile. After the Jews had rejected the Gospel of Christ as a nation, the Gospel was carried into the world for the Gentiles as well; and so the church was established among non-Jews all over the world. Paul the chief apostle of the early church era became the foremost messenger of the Gospel to the Gentiles. With the church well established among the Gentiles, Paul reports that another house of God was now found upon the foundation of Christ. Not a house of the seed of Abraham, but of the seed of Christ. Two different households are now in effect: The house of Israel and the house of Christ. In Ephesians, chapter 2, Paul calls the church of Christ, "FELLOW CITIZENS" of the household of God, no longer to be strangers and foreigners. In the book of Galatians, the Apostle Paul calls the church the "HOUSEHOLD OF FAITH" (Gal. 6:10).

As we study the 2000-year history of the church, we are able to distinguish two peak periods of great revival, prominence and influence upon society. The first period of revival (known as the FORMER RAIN) was the era of the first generation of the church, stretching from Pentecost until the death of the last apostles of the first church. The second period (known as THE LATTER RAIN) is in the time of the final generation of the church, which based upon biblical calculations of the times and seasons is "THE PRESENT ONE." The prophecy of Haggai talks about a "HOUSE" and distinguishes both a "FORMER" and a "LATTER" house. Once again the former and latter house prophecies portray a truth which applies to both Israel and the church, yet at "DIFFERENT TIME PERIODS." The first generation of the church was clearly the former house, and the final generation of the church is evidently going to be the latter house of the church. Regarding the nation of Israel, the application of the former house and the latter house is a somewhat different story. The former house referred to here in Haggai, chapter 2, was the first temple of Israel which was built by the great King Solomon. The latter house is the very temple which the Jews were struggling to build at this time of the prophecy. We know from the context of the prophecy that God promises Israel, that the glory of this new temple under construction would be greater than the former temple of Solomon. And so history confirms that it was indeed so. But during the lifetime of Jesus and His ministry on the earth, the temple situation clearly changes. The latter temple of Zerubbabel now becomes the former temple, since Jesus begins to talk about a new or latter temple to come in the future.

On several occasions Jesus Himself also prophesied of the doom and destruction of this temple. He was also quick to agree with the prophet Daniel that in the last days, a new temple would be built. This third and final temple is the one that will be inaugurated at the beginning of the seven-year tribulation period, immediately succeeding the rapture of the church. Israel will then resume the sacrifice order of the temple, worshipping God in accordance with the old covenant rituals of temple worship. This religious returning to Judaism will commence on the same day as the rapture of the church, which is the first day of the seven years of tribulation. This third temple is the one which the antichrist will defile and horrendously dishonour for 1260 days, or the latter 3.5 years of the tribulation period. But it is also the same temple that Jesus will cleanse after defeating the antichrist in battle. Jesus will then reign over Israel from this third temple for 1000 years. So the new end-time temple structure which Israel will construct in the near future now becomes the "LATTER HOUSE OF THE LAST DAYS OF ISRAEL."

THE GOLD

Gold has always been a representation of God because of its beauty, purity, and preciousness as a commodity of wealth. Since the days of Abraham, gold represented wealth and riches. The Book of Genesis mentions certain transactions of business which were substantiated in gold. Today gold is still the backbone of our wealth. The wealth of the world is measured in gold, and the money we use is backed by gold reserves. Because of its exceptional beauty, gold was used as ornaments with jewels, and became the reason for our being adorned in it today. When Israel departed from the land of Egypt, the Israelites received precious metals such as silver and gold from the Egyptians in great abundance; and stripped Egypt, the world empire of the day, of all her wealth. While Israel had journeyed through the wilderness, God commanded Moses to build Him a tabernacle where He may come and dwell, so that He may be among His people. Upon completion of the tabernacle, God's glorious presence filled and occupied the holy of holies of the tabernacle. The tabernacle was to be constructed from the free will offerings which the people were requested to bring to Moses. This temple offering brought in by the people should consist of GOLD, silver, bronze, a selection of linen thread, goat's hair, and ram's skin, including a few minor important materials.

A study of Exodus, chapters 25-30, reveals the lavish and unrestrained usage of GOLD in the tabernacle. Nearly every commodity used to furnish the tabernacle was either made out of pure solid gold, or it was overlaid and covered with gold. The word "GOLD" appears no less than 42 times in this passage, and is used every time concerning the furnishing of something for the tabernacle. No wonder Israel's enemies would always go straight for the temple in Jerusalem during an invasion. (The temple was like the local bank in the center of town in the wild west movies.) It was the STOREHOUSE. Literally, it was the place where all the gold and riches of the nation was "STORED" as ornaments and furniture of the temple. Please study this passage of Scripture as it is far too lengthy to print. Note the frequent usage of the word "GOLD" and also the phrase "PURE GOLD." The tabernacle was completely filled with gold. By stockpiling the tabernacle and later the temple with gold, God was trying to convey a special message to Israel. The message was a simple one: Israel must fill the tabernacle or temple with GOLD, whereafter God would fill it with GLORY. Bear in mind that the mercy seat with its two golden cherubim angels on both ends of the mercy seat were also made out of pure gold (Ex. 25:17-18). When the divine presence of God descended from above and filled the holy of holies, residing in a place of suspension above the mercy seat in midair, midway between the two cherubims on both ends of the mercy seat, God's presence of GLORY dwelt amidst the GOLD. The "GLORY" of God came to rest above the golden mercy seat and its two cherubims. Immediately beneath the actual resting place of the presence of God was GOLD (the mercy seat). On both the left and the right side of God's presence were GOLDEN cherubim. God's presence of GLORY would have been totally surrounded by GOLD had it not been for the opening on the top (above), heavenward, which was deliberately left that way so that God's presence could travel down into that position.

Here in the tabernacle, we have God's divine presence surrounded by gold: on the left is GOLD; on the right is GOLD; beneath it is GOLD; and in the middle between all the gold is GLORY; only the upward direction was kept clear. God surrounded Himself in the tabernacle with GOLD. GLORY and GOLD became the two most important commodities of the tabernacle and later on in the temple in Jerusalem. In all this, there is a very important lesson for us to learn. God's plan with the tabernacle and later the temple in Jerusalem sends a strong message to His people which requires a great lesson to be learned. Here are three facts to be observed about the gold in the temple:

1. GOD LIKES GOLD.

God is the one who has created the gold of the earth, ALL of it. None of it evolved by chance. The Lord placed the gold of earth at our disposal so that we may become rich with it and be reminded by the gold itself, that God is full of riches and glory. God wanted Israel to "STOCKPILE" the tabernacle and temple with gold so that the rich presence of gold would always serve as a reminder of the fact that God likes gold! God's house shall be a house of gold. "GOD LIKES GOLD!" God likes the gold so much that He was prepared to manifest His own presence into a gold-filled room on the earth, and that was long before Jesus had come to sanctify the earth with His work of redemption. The earthly sanctuary of the temple was a replica of the heavenly, where God is also encompassed about with gold upon the throne of heaven. The streets of heaven also are paved and filled with gold. Back on earth, the Christian's trial of faith is about the only thing that is more precious than gold. We need to realize this truth. "GOD LIKES GOLD." God has filled His universe with gold.

2. GOLD AND GLORY BELONG TOGETHER IN THE HOUSE OF GOD.

Gold and glory belong in the house of God. That is their place in God's house. Not among the heathen, but in God's house. Israel is responsible for bringing the gold into the house, and God is responsible for bringing the glory into the house. Israel's part is the gold, God's part is the glory. In those days, the glory of God was not available to sinful man. NO! God's presence had to be securely contained only in the house of God; in the holy of holies. Likewise the gold was not to be squandered on the streets or in the marketplaces, No! The gold was almost like a "HOLY COMMODITY" reserved only for the house of God where His presence dwelt amongst the gold. Together, the gold and glory inhabited the house of God. Since those early days, gold and glory were inseparable in the house of God. They were like inseparable twins. They belonged in God's house, and they belonged together. The gold and glory. THEY ARE INSEPARABLE TWINS OF GOD'S MERCY.

3. SEPARATING THE GOLD FROM THE GLORY RESULTS IN THE DEPARTURE OF GOD.

If the gold and the glory were to be separated, one from the other, such separation would bring the curse upon Israel. The specific curse was POVERTY. The glory of God's presence in the temple would assure God's protection and forgiveness of sins. The gold would assure Israel of prosperity and wealth, which served as a token of God's prosperity as well as being a seed of prosperity sown in the house of God, since Israel had brought the gold for the temple as a love offering of giving.

In the temple of Israel, the Gold was a "REQUIRE-MENT" while the glory was an "ENDOWMENT." Israel brought the gold and God furnished the glory. Over in the New Testament the same thing is still true and remains in effect. God wants to fill the New Testament church also with an abundance of gold and glory. The only difference lies in the reversed order of the gold and the glory for the New Testament church. Prior to His departure, Jesus promised His disciples His glory (John 17:22). Prior to His ascension, the Lord promised an outpouring of God's glory in the person of the Holy Spirit. On the day of Pentecost, the glory of God began to be poured out upon the followers of Jesus. But the blessings of Abraham are transferred to the church through Jesus, and the church becomes heirs of God and joint heirs with Jesus our Lord. The New Testament is a covenant of glory and gold. First the glory, then the gold.

GOLD AND GLORY IN GOD'S WORD

A fine thread of the message of the gold and the glory weaves its way through the Scriptures. Beginning with Abraham, God initially offered him friendship and promised him wealth in the same breath. We see the same truth in the lives of Isaac and Jacob. When Israel departed Egypt for the promised land, she stripped the Egyptians of all their gold and wealth before embarking on their journey. After Israel had crossed the Jordan to begin the reoccupation of the land, she engaged in warfare on numerous occasions, always seizing the wealth of her enemies in battle. As long as Israel abided in the glory, God kept adding the gold. Solomon, the wisest man ever, and king of Israel, was offered wealth and riches by God as one of his choices. When he selected wisdom, God threw in the wealth as a bonus anyway. Solomon chose the glory and got the gold as well. In the book of Matthew, Jesus delivers a very profound teaching concerning wealth and glory (Matt. 6:25-33). In verse 32 He tells us not to seek after the gold (material possessions of the world). The Gentiles live that way. In verse 33 Jesus tells us to seek the kingdom of God and its righteousness (the glory). So, if we seek after the glory of God first, then He will simply add the gold (wealth), and everything we may need or desire. But the glory comes first. The glory of God is what we should set our hearts upon, not the gold. If our priorities are correct, and we seek God's glory, then He will automatically add the gold. We should not seek after the wealth of this world, NO! We should rather seek the presence of God. Then the Lord Himself will take care of the gold!

I do not want anyone reading this book to get the wrong impression. This message is not for fortune hunters, or for those who are looking for a way to get rich quick! NO! God is after your heart, which should then bring a longing in your life for His glory and presence. I am not teaching people to seek after wealth like the world does. NO! This chapter will verify the fact that walking in close fellowship with God every day is the key to wealth; first spiritual, then financial and material wealth. Once again the gold and the glory accompany each other, and flow completely together. I wish Christians will learn this great truth. We say we believe it but we really do not. Most Christians are so busy trying to make money they have no time to seek the things of God. And then there are Christians that sit at home all day, confessing Scriptures a thousand times a day for their prosperity. I wish they would get up and go out on the streets and preach the Gospel and attend to the needs of others, then they will see the hand of God move to prosper them and make them rich. Why? Because Jesus told us to SEEK THE GLORY by seeking His kingdom. Seek after the glory and God will send you the gold! Seek after the things of God, and God will seek after your desires and well-being.

Jesus also warned us not to store up our treasures on earth, but in heaven, where the true riches are heaven's gold and glory. Jesus also judged people's spiritual maturity (degree of glory) by what they gave financially into the work of God (amount of gold sown.) Today people's spiritual maturity level is judged not by what they give into the kingdom, but by how much they possess. When people have four Cadillacs in the driveway of their mansion, and are sitting in the elders pew on Sunday, people think that they must be very spiritual. The truth really in my experience is that those people are usually stingy, very manipulative and controlling people, always striving with the pastor, always trying to bind up the church and the pastor with their devilish, cunning and crafty schemes. NO!! That's not spiritual at all. The amount of gold you possess does not determine your spiritual state of existence. Definitely not. Jesus judged spirituality by what you give, not by what you own. Remember the widow who put one mite in the treasury of the temple? Jesus said that she had given more than anybody else, because she gave ALL SHE HAD!

In the Book of Acts we observe the gold and glory principle in chapter 4. While the disciples were praying earnestly after being threatened by the authorities, the "GLORY" of God shook the building with great power, followed by the performance of signs and wonders by the apostles. THE GLORY MADE WAY FOR THE GOLD! The believers came together in one accord in the glory of God, went out afterwards and sold their possessions, and brought the money (gold) into the house of God and there was an abundance of gold also in the house of God. The glory came in first, followed by the gold. In 1 Corinthians, chapter 9, Paul asks the question whether it would be asking too much, if we sow the Gospel (glory) and then reap material things (gold) from the people. In 2 Corinthians, chapter 8:9, Paul tells us that part of the work of grace on the cross (glory), was for Jesus to become poor for us so that we through Christ's poverty could become rich (gold). In 2 Corinthians 9:7-8, Paul tells us that the generous giving of our finances (gold) would release the grace of God (glory) towards us. Even in the familiar trend of Philippians 4 the same is still true. Paul talks about the sowing of finances into his ministry (gold), and says in verse 19, that, having sown "GOLD" into his ministry, that God will supply their needs according to His riches in "GLORY" by Christ Jesus.

As we page through the Word of God the list goes on and on. The GLORY AND THE GOLD go together in the Gospel message, Old and New Testament. *THE GLORY AND THE GOLD BELONG TOGETHER IN THE HOUSEHOLD OF GOD.*

JEWS, GENTILES AND THE CHURCH

According to 1 Corinthians 10:32, God divides all people into three different categories or groups of people namely: Jews, Gentiles and the church of God. When we examine people's viewpoint regarding finances, the same thing is true. The Jews know their spiritual heritage; that they are the children of Abraham, and that their covenant with God unequivocally entitles them to wealth and prosperity. If you ever try to convince them otherwise you are wasting your time, and you will be met with an unshakable confidence. The Jews KNOW who they are! They KNOW that they have an everlasting covenant of prosperity with their God. It is impossible to sway them to accept anything else. The results are proof enough. Jews are rich, like their Father Abraham. No poverty for the Jews, that's for sure!

Now let's talk about the second category of people, the Gentiles, called the heathen, the unsaved, or the ungodly. The ungodly around us refuse to believe that poverty is a good thing. They spend their entire life almost working themselves to death to try and make more money. They know rich is better than poor. Not having any spiritual perception, they rely on common sense that says: Rich is good, poor is not! Money can buy the things we have need of in everyday life. Money pays the bills. Money keeps the "WOLVES" away from the door. Money is a gift in this life. Money is a good thing, and poverty is a terrible threat to life! This is the way unsaved or ungodly people view money. It is definitely a good thing to them, which they endeavour to pursue diligently everyday. Some people will sell their souls for money, others will lie, steal, cheat and even murder to obtain more money. The world seeks after money everyday with a passion, in legitimate ways as well as in the most illegitimate and crooked ways. The world believes and knows that "MONEY IS A GOOD THING."

The only people in society who can be convinced to believe that money is a bad and evil thing are thousands of born-again God-loving sincere ignorant Christian people belonging to the ranks of the church. Many of us, however, have awakened to this truth already, having learned the wonderful biblical truth of God's prosperity and financial blessings for us, as promised in His Word. But there are multitudes of Christians who continue to hold on to the old-time outdated unscriptural doctrines of poverty. They still believe the unscriptural lie about being humble and poor, cleaving to all those ridiculous doctrines of poverty which we have just exposed as being false in a previous chapter. No wonder so many Christians have come to believe this poverty garbage! The poverty faction of the church is the only group of people in society who actually believe that poverty is a blessing, and that prosperity is a curse and is something to be avoided at all costs.

SEPARATING THE GOLD AND THE GLORY

God has always intended for the gold and the glory to be like inseparable twins in His earthly house. The devil, therefore, was left with no alternative but to severely challenge this powerful dual of God's blessings. For Satan, an attack on the gold and glory combination in God's house was a matter of life or death.

Starting on the day of Pentecost, the church immediately became Satan's target concerning an attempt to separate the gold and the glory in God's house. It did not take the devil long after Pentecost to get on the inside to do his destructive work. In Acts, chapter 2, the glory of God fell in the upper room. In the very next chapter we can see that the devil had already infiltrated the church by challenging God's glory with poverty. In Acts, chapter 3, we read the story of Peter and John, being confronted by a beggar at the gate of the temple. When the beggar asked the two apostles for money, Peter responded by declaring proudly that he had no possession of either silver or GOLD. Peter did not possess any gold, but he did have an abundant provision of glory. What did the lame man actually need? Gold or glory? The answer is twofold. He was in need of the GLORY first, in order to receive a miracle of healing. But then he also was in need of a financial miracle (gold) since he had been devastated by poverty! He needed BOTH! GLORY AND GOLD! He got the GLORY, and he got healed! But he remained poor and destitute financially. Yet the healing and the prosperity are supposed to go together. The GOLD and the GLORY GO TOGETHER! But the devil had already succeeded in separating the gold from the glory in the newfound church of Jesus.

For the two disciples Peter and John, the emphasis on the newfound GLORY was strongly intact. But the usual 2000-year-old emphasis of the sons of Abraham on the GOLD was suddenly gone. In actual fact, since the Holy Spirit was poured out upon Peter, he had already given up his inheritance of prosperity as a son of Abraham! The same thing has continued to happen to Christians throughout the 2000-year history of the church. As soon as the Holy Spirit is poured out and a new revival breaks forth, the church forgets about the gold, so the devil rapidly moves in and steals whatever finances and material possessions we have left. Instead of the church combining the gold and the glory together, especially during revival, we allow the devil to steal the gold while we are enjoying the glory. Be on the lookout, dear Christian, when you are having revival and enjoying the GLORY of God, the devil will try to steal the gold in the house. The bulk of all the wealth of the church, however, was stolen long ago! This happened back during the beginning days of the early church. The devil put together a master plan to separate the gold from the glory in the early church and we are still suffering the effects of that deal today, while hell is still enjoying the benefits of this 2000-year-old deal, which was originally made with the church of the Book of Acts. Let us consider the full story of that tragedy. Here is a hypothetical illustration of what I believe the devil did when he "signed a business deal" with the early church.

THE DEVIL'S CONTRACT WITH THE CHURCH

I am convinced that the devil signed a financial contract with the early church. I can just imagine the devil with his big pot belly, puffing on a big cigar, coming to Jerusalem to attend a special meeting with the church. The devil made sure that he was armed securely with a pack of lies in his briefcase for this business meeting. What he was about to do was to sell a bunch of lies to Peter and the other apostles. First the devil must have praised them by saying that the glory of God in their ministries was wonderful and that not even he would attempt to deny the fact that the church had gained the upper hand in their struggle. He further proceeded to say that the church was in grave danger of losing the anointing of God and the signs and wonders in their ministries, because the gold was going to pervert and spoil them, and that the riches of this world would turn them away from the anointing of the Holy Spirit. The wealth of this world would also cause the apostles to be lifted up in pride, robbing them of the humility that servants of God of their caliber ought to have at all times.

The devil continued to pour out his sermon of lies, preaching one lie after the other, until he had finally sold them on his idea. Having wounded the apostles of the Lord like a deer in the woods, it was now time for the kill. So he jumped up from the board room table, stooped over Peter's chair and landed his proposal on the table in front of him. This proposal was simple and downright to the point. It stated that if the church would be prepared to give the gold and the wealth of the earth to the devil for safekeeping, the church could then hang on to the glory. In other words, Satan would take the gold, and they (the church), can keep the glory. An equal split. If this agreement could be reached, the devil promised that he would not bother the church any more, but leave her alone to preach the Gospel and do the work of the ministry. As long as he could keep the gold, the church could do whatever they wished with the rest.

The apostles were all in agreement with this proposal and applauded the devil, and thanked him for such a "fair and decent offer." "We do not want the money any way," Peter probably said. "It is really none of our concern what you do with the money, just as long as you leave us alone, so that we can get on with the preaching of the Gospel!" It was an absolute deal. Caught by Satan's snare, the church sold out the gold to the devil, renouncing all the wealth of the earth. The devil's doctrines against the dangers of gold (wealth) for the church were then unanimously adopted by the church as her own doctrines against wealth. The devil's sermon entitled "the dangers of wealth" had become the doctrine of poverty for the church. These lies, recorded on Satan's contract with the church, are still being preached in churches all over the world and believed on, while the devil is laughing at us. The devil got the gold, the church and the glory!

There was just one thing the devil forgot to mention during his business meeting with the church leaders. It is called "THE GOSPEL VEHICLE." The message of the Gospel vehicle was not known by the church at the time of signing the devil's contract of poverty. You see, without the gold, you cannot spread the glory for too long. When your resources run out, the preaching of the Gospel stops. So the devil got back into his helicopter, flew back to hell and threw a big party. Back in hell the devil said, "I'VE GOT MYSELF A HELL OF A DEAL" and laughed his head off. "Now the church will never be able to preach the Gospel to the whole world!" HA, HA, HA, HA! And he laughed, and laughed, and is still laughing today. But thank God, that grin is about to be wiped off his face soon. The church is almost done with singing songs like, "I'm just a beggar in the heat and the cold," and "I'm just a pilgrim in a land that is not my own," and other lyrics of doom and poverty. The devil's party is almost over forever, and the church is about to be delivered supernaturally from the 2000-year curse of poverty. Hallelujah!

CHURCH POVERTY

Concerning the GOLD and the GLORY, there are four different types of churches.

1. THE TRADITIONAL CHURCH

This kind of church has been without the glory of God for hundreds of years. There are no signs and wonders, no manifestation of God and no presence of the Holy Spirit's anointing. It is dead. NO GLORY! Nothing. The doctrine of poverty which has created a false humility is flourishing, and there is plenty of poverty. NO GOLD. The place is dead. There is no glory and absolutely no gold. It's a cemetery. It's history.

2. THE PENTECOSTAL CHURCH

Here you find some happy clappers, with tongues and prophecy. Once in a while someone gets delivered or healed in the service and the people shout and rejoice. Very exciting! HERE'S SOME GLORY! But as soon as you start talking about money, they throw you out because in the presence of God is no room for the things of this world. NO GOLD, they say. Here we find some glory, but definitely no gold.

3. THE CHARISMATIC CHURCH

Here they sing all the right songs, know all the right Scriptures and say all the right things. But it's become a formula. There's no anointing, and the Holy Spirit does not fall. No signs and wonders. NO GLORY! Yet when you talk to the people you find some prosperity there. Wrongfully they believe prosperity is measured by what you possess, and obtained by what you confess, but it's not. But at least there is some prosperity and it is welcome. So you will find some gold in the house, but no glory!

4. THE PROPHETIC CHURCH

This is the church of the future. A church that will abound in both the glory and gold of God.

The glory will be received by people walking in the anointing, filled to overflowing with God's presence. Signs and wonders will be the order of the day. The Holy Spirit will be in complete control, and His fire will direct us in God's perfect will everyday. Joel's army of fire shall be raised up and prevail. And the glory of God will usher in the gold, and the house of God shall be filled with glory and gold in abundance. And the Lord shall be glorified!

The biggest mistake ever committed by the church has been our rejection of the person of the Holy Spirit. Oftentimes Christians condemn the Jews for rejecting Jesus as Messiah, yet we have rejected the Spirit of God as Jesus' "SUBSTITUTE." In 1987 we began to see a fresh move of the Spirit of God in our meetings. Today it is called "THE LAUGHTER REVIVAL or TORONTO BLESSING or REVIVAL OF JOY." Yet the point is that, overwhelmingly, the so-called "CHARIS-MATIC" church has rejected this wonderful visitation of God. Many have entered in, yet many others are not interested, because their hearts are not hungry for God. People still find some kind of fault with it and steer away from it. This is a pattern in the church. From the time of the Pentecostal revival of 1906, Christians have continually rejected the move of God in recent times. For this reason each of these revivals had to flourish outside the church, in tents and auditoriums. What a shame. Due to this fact, we have reaped the fruit of an ever-increasing POVERTY in the house of God.

We have not yet learned that the anointing and the financial blessings of God go hand in hand. The more of the presence of God I receive, the more prosperity will flow into my life. It is the same story of the gold and the glory. The gold and the glory go together. We've been in some meetings where the power of God would fall and people would end up being carried out drunk in the Holy Ghost, yet the place is half-full. This proves to me that the church has not yet learned the truth nor experienced the power of the GOLD and the GLORY, in knowing that they are inseparable twins of God's blessings. If they had, the house would be full, every night, night after night. The prayer lines would be busy all night long and people would flock to the front every night, at ANY invitation. But the sorrowful truth re-mains. Many of our glory and gold services are not packed out with people yet, because the church is still ignorant of this divine truth. Now have an altar call for healing and finances, and everybody and his dog is there. Call for people to get filled and drunk in the Spirit, and many shine in their absence. How dumb can you get! When are God's people going to learn the truth? "THE GLORY AND GOLD GO TOGETHER!" The more GLORY you receive, the more GOLD you receive. The more of God's presence, the more of His blessings. Psalm 16:11 speaks this great revelation of the prosperity of the gold and the glory, "...In Your presence is fullness of joy..." it says. What an incredible revelation of financial prosperity. It says that there is fullness of joy in the presence of the Lord. People say, "But that verse says nothing about finances, money or wealth!" Oh yes it does! In the presence of the Lord is FULLNESS! I know that it continues to say "fullness of joy," but the entrance into God's presence usually BEGINS with joy, that is supernatural joy, and an outpouring of it. This is not talking about a mental state of joy that we may aspire to, NO! It is referring to an outpouring of God's supernatural joy within us, which will result in a bursting forth of laughter, jubilance, drunkenness in the Spirit, and other "MANIFESTATIONS" of the Holy Spirit through us.

These wonderful manifestations of the Holy Spirit gave birth to the Pentecostal churches at the turn of the century. Such works of the Holy Spirit are still resisted by the church community today, Pentecostal and non-Pentecostals alike. The difference between most Pentecostal and charismatic churches as opposed to the mainline traditional churches are becoming fewer by the day. In most instances you can hardly tell any difference at all. The one is as dead as the other. Some so-called Pentecostal churches might as well put a traditional name on the door instead of the name of their Pentecostal or charismatic denomination. At least they will attract more members that way. Our barrenness in the presence and move of the Holy Spirit has brought lack and poverty into Pentecostal and charismatic churches. But in God's actual MANIFEST PRESENCE is FULLNESS OF NOT ONLY JOY, BUT FULLNESS OF EVERYTHING GOD HAS! The fullness starts with joy; once we have fully entered into His joy, and end up drunk and jubilant in the Spirit, ALL of the fullness of God becomes available to us. But it only becomes available when we enter INTO THE SPIRIT! Not by staying high and dry in the flesh. Once we have entered into His presence, all of God's fullness miraculously becomes available to us to receive in the Spirit.

We need to understand that God is the ETERNAL SOURCE of life and all things. When we enter into the presence of the Spirit of God, we come in close personal contact with the SOURCE of all things: God Himself! When we touch the SOURCE, God releases the RESOURCE. In other words, when we come into God's presence, we will find the fullness for everything that we can imagine or dream of. If the totality of all resources are not to be found in God's presence, where could it ever be? Remember, GOD IS THE SOURCE OF ALL CREATION! If something could not be found in God's presence, it does not EXIST! GET INTO GOD'S PRESENCE! If you have no passion for the anointing of the Holy Spirit, and no hunger for His touch, then get into the presence of God at least for financial gain. Perhaps God will have mercy and let you be blessed financially if nothing else. But once you have tasted of heavenly wine, you will come back everyday for more and more, not seeking the gold, but longing for the sweetness and ecstasy of His glory. When will we ever learn that the GOLD and the GLORY of God flow together in the house of God? And in the fullness of God's presence is FULLNESS OF EVERYTHING THAT GOD POSSESSES.

The proof of the pudding is in the eating. Our office receives letters everyday from people who have come into the anointing of God in our meetings whose financial status have drastically improved since their encounter with God. Some of the results are absolutely miraculous. Time and space would not allow me to relate some of these incredible stories to you. The overwhelming evidence is solid proof to the fact that "the proof of the pudding is in the eating," and that the eating has been sweet for many people, after they were blessed with the overflow of God's Spirit in the meetings. The GOLD and the GLORY go together in the house of the Lord. Every good and perfect gift comes from God, and in the presence of the Lord is FULLNESS. I pray to God that His people would wake up in this hour and come into His Glory. God is the SOURCE of all things. He is prosperity personified.

We need to abandon all our own ideas, plans and programs, and accept God's plan unconditionally. Then we will enter into a glory unknown and see the manifestation of prosperity never imagined before. Let's get into revival and into the flow of the anointing! Let's get filled up with God's presence repeatedly and drink of the Spirit every day and so obey the instruction of the Lord Jesus to us. Let's get drunk in the Spirit, and let God bless us with wealth, spiritually and materially, GOLD and GLORY! The house of God is a place of gold and glory. And in these last days God is going to bring both the gold and the glory into the end-time church of revival. Like Paul says in Romans 13:11, "...it is high time to awake out of sleep..." because everything that God wants to do in these last days including financially is now nearer than when we first believed. Now is the time for the church to stop playing religious games, and begin to hunger after the presence and the manifestations of God! It is time for us to get out of

God's way, and let the Holy Spirit do the work of heaven amongst us. It is time to stop criticizing the move of God, and get into the flow. Jesus did not invite us who are "THIRSTY" to come to Him and "THINK." NO! We should come and DRINK! That is, drink the Holy Spirit! REMEMBER, the more we drink of His Spirit, the more we can be filled. The more we are filled with God's presence, the more fullness we will enter into! It is that simple, yet that profound! The more glory we receive, the more gold we'll obtain. When we freely receive the glory all the time, God will freely manifest the gold. The end-time prophetic church of glory and gold is about to rise and fulfill the words of Haggai the prophet, because the prophetic hour of the church of gold and glory will very soon arrive, THANK GOD! This is the hour ordained of God, and nothing and nobody will stop it. The gold and the glory will flow back into the house of God, and the Lord will be well pleased with His people!

5 | *God's Holy Ghost Hamburger Idea...*

"I wisdom dwell with prudence, and find out knowledge of witty inventions." Proverbs 8:12, KJV

The supernatural ability of God placed within every born-again human spirit, to enable every believer to hear the voice of God, lies at the heart of the message of this chapter. Individually, Christians today need to seek after that special personal experience, of encountering the Person of the Holy Spirit face to face, discovering Him intimately and personally. I am not talking about a doctrine, a prayer or a Scripture confession. I am talking about a living encounter with the bigger-than-life personality of the living Holy Spirit of God. Few Christians in modern times have succeeded in their quest to discover the Holy Spirit personally because they have been hampered in their search by religious doctrines and attitudes which have bound the church for many years. But for those who were successful, their friendship with the Holy Spirit has made Him more real to them than any physical person they know on earth. For the believer who succeeds in their quest after the Holy Spirit, the unlimited realms of God's creative power will become available to them through the VOICE of the Holy Spirit, speaking His words of life to them....If we learn how to successfully interact with the person of the Holy Spirit in these last days, and learn to walk sensitively to His influence in our lives and get to know His voice speaking to us from the heart of God, we will succeed in this message called "GOD'S HOLY GHOST HAMBURGER IDEA."

Of these fivefold multiple blessings of prosperity for the end-time church, everyone will come to us in a SUPERNATURAL way. That means God will initiate and perform the miraculous works HIMSELF. On the other hand, we always have a part to play, sometimes it may be more and other times less. In the case of this fourth financial wonder of the last day church, our part to play is BIGGER than in all of the other four events. The Holy Ghost hamburger idea is like a seed that is sown into our spirit when the Spirit of God communicates it to us, and once received, the battle is half won. Simple faith in the supernaturally communicated seed will enable us to rise to the occasion and act in accordance with what we have received, through the voice of the Holy Spirit. Our responsibility concerning the Holy Ghost hamburger venture consists of two parts. The first part is to HEAR CORRECTLY from the Holy Spirit, and the second part is to ACT APPROPRIATELY, and in accordance with what we have heard from the Holy Spirit. First is "HEARING," then second comes "ACTING."

At the same time, there are enormous obstacles in the way of the realization of the hamburger idea in these last days. Even though every born-again believer possesses the God-given ability to hear the voice of the

Holy Spirit speaking to us within our spirit man, it takes years of close fellowship with the Holy Spirit on a daily basis to develop this "spiritual endowment" into an "art of divine communication." But the modern-day church focuses on quantity instead of quality, therefore, our present-day church environment, is not an environment of sensitivity or of being yielded to the person of the Holy Spirit, nor does it lend itself to the distinguishing art of hearing the Spirit's voice. Ministers such as Benny Hinn have strived for years with the message of the Holy Spirit and His person, trying to bring about an awareness of the Spirit's presence, and perhaps trigger a revival or a rediscovering of the reality of the Holy Spirit among today's Christians. But traditions are strong, and the return of the church to the person of the Holy Spirit has only just begun.

Almost every born-again Christian living in this crucial final hour of the church qualifies for the hamburger idea, and becomes a candidate for its multiple blessings. Three things are required for anybody to become a candidate for the hamburger idea:

1. You need to be alive and well at present (this is the final generation of the church).

2. You must be born again, which legitimately places you in the body of Christ.

3. Your occupation as a Christian must be anything other than that of a full-time fivefold minister in the body of Christ (which in most cases will disqualify you for an extended business venture). So the QUALIFICATION part is easy. It is the APPROPRIATION part that seems impossible, unless, if we comply with the following four requirements of God. Study these four points listed below very carefully, because they will open the way for us to the hamburger idea. We must travel their path of wisdom in order for us to reach the hamburger idea in the fu-

ture. These four qualifications for the appropriation of the hamburger idea will revolutionize your entire walk with God IF you begin to follow after them diligently. These four points are hidden in the secret place of the most high, and they who begin to dwell in that secret place will learn the great truths of these four secrets to the hamburger idea.

HAMBURGER SECRETS

Here are the four great secrets to the hamburger idea.

1. You have to discover the great person of the Holy Spirit FOR YOURSELF through a personal experience with God. You cannot live by Benny Hinn's experience. That's second hand to you. You MUST have your own "BURNING BUSH EXPERIENCE" with God.

2. Once you have discovered the Holy Spirit for yourself, you must cultivate this newfound personal relationship through daily fellowship and communication with the Holy Spirit as a person. The relationship will then develop into a wonderful intimate friendship with the Holy Spirit.

3. Everyday friendship with the Holy Spirit will produce a closeness and a sensitivity in your spirit to the voice of the Holy Spirit. After this, hearing and responding to the voice of the Spirit will become easy and spontaneous. Maintaining a daily friendship with him will keep you "TUNED IN" to the Spirit's heartbeat at all times, so that when He begins to speak to you, you will immediately recognize His already familiar voice, and distinguish exactly what He says to you, so that you may know what to do

about it. There will come a time when His voice will be as familiar to you as any human person, except that His voice is far more precious than anyone else. The guidance of the Holy Spirit will now become part of everyday life.

4. When the Holy Spirit finally speaks the *hamburger idea* to your heart, you will recognize the ever-so-familiar voice of the Spirit immediately, and rise up in simple faith to carrry out the instructions that He has given you to the end or to the fulfillment of the assignment of the hamburger idea. HALLELUJAH!

Here are the four hamburger secrets summarized:

1. Discover the Holy Spirit personally.

2. Establish a relationship with Him through daily fellowship.

3. Develop a close friendship with the Holy Spirit, while you learn the secret of listening to His voice daily.

4. Respond immediately to the voice of the Spirit, promptly carrying out His secret instructions spoken to you.

These four hamburger secrets might seem easy to carry out in our quest for the hamburger idea, but unfortunately the path is filled with many obstacles or cheap substitutes of Christianity.

CHEAP SUBSTITUTES

The practice of cheap substitutes in the church today has robbed God's people of the opportunity to discover the depth of the Spirit life with all its wonderful blessings. Oftentimes, the gold of the Spirit life is substituted for the cheaper commodity of brass. After all, it LOOKS the same, and it SHINES the same as the gold, but in reality it is far removed from it. If we fail to strike gold in the Sunday morning service, we just seem to settle easily for a chunk of worthless brass. When the real anointing of "gold" fails to show up, we quickly produce some "brass" after the flesh, and present it to the people as "gold." But it's worthless. The brass at large has completely substituted the gold in the church in our day. But most of us are convinced that it is in fact "gold." But it is not.

Two kinds of cheap substitutes of brass can be found in our churches today. The first kind is a "WORLDLY" practice or substitute, while the second kind is a "RELIGIOUS" practice or substitute. Both of them are equally dangerous and detrimental to spiritual health.

Worldliness has always posed a threat to true spirituality. World-like attitudes and habits always seem to creep into our churches from time to time. But presently, they flourish in the courts of the Lord. But since they are brass and without any value, they produce poverty after their own kind. The cheap substitute of worldiness causes the church to pattern things after the ways of the world. Presently, the church is almost under the spell of the world, greatly influenced by her, politically and socially alike. The church is certainly not turning the world upsidedown, instead, the world is turning the church upsidedown with her strong influence over the church. The absence of a geniune move of the Holy Spirit in the church for several decades has made the church increasingly susceptible to the influences of the world system. The church has become imitators of the world, instead of imitators of God. The church is being conformed to the world, subsequently, we are constantly trying to do things like the world, because that is the popular "NORM" of society. We write the same kind of songs they write, and sing them the same way without the anointing.We preach a socially accepted message not to offend anyone. We try to be VISITOR FRIENDLY, instead of showing no compromise for the power of the Gospel. We have changed the conduct of our church services to look like a secular music concert, so that everyone would feel "AT HOME" should they show up. In some instances, the church is no longer a Christian center, but an entertainment center. The entire church service from beginning to end is just a "SHOW," filled with worldly substitutes throughout its entire duration.

The second kind of cheap substitutes, namely the religious ones, are equally lethal to spiritual health in the church. Religious practices are spiritual rituals which have a form of godliness, yet they have no power nor life to them. They form a sequence of dumb dead rituals, which we call the "PROGRAM" of the church service. This rich heritage of religious practices have completely substituted the presence and power of the Holy Spirit in the church world. Consequently, all the brass, whether religious or worldly, have enforced the grip of poverty upon the church like a deadly stronghold.

I urge you to consider the following five cheap substitutes in the church, and decide for yourself whether they are worthy to rob us any longer of the glorious life of the Spirit, including keeping the door shut on us concerning the hamburger venture of blessing!

The first two cheap substitutes are worldly ones, followed by three more which are religious ones. It is time to remove the obstacles of cheap substitutes presently in our way, since at present, they make the blessing of this chapter unobtainable.

1. THE SUPERFICIAL CHURCH

There remains a vast difference between the modern-day church as opposed to the early church of the Book of Acts. The early church was full of *power, glory and Holy Spirit* REVIVAL. The present-day church in contrast with the early one is a church of organization, constitutionalism and regimentation. The spiritual condition of the modern-day church can be contrasted with the early church as follows: "The first church was Holy Ghost controlled, and the present-day church is man controlled." The change over from Holy Spirit control to the other extreme of humanistic control was indeed a gradual process. After the first century had ended, and the early apostles had died, the church began to forfeit the dominance of the Spirit by substituting the initiative and control maintained by the Holy Spirit in the church for man's ideas. Today this trend of humanism is still greatly preferred at large, even in so-called "Holy Ghost" churches around the world, because God's people still prefer to be dignified before man instead of being "GLORIFIED" in the Spirit. Many of the church services can be preprogrammed on the computer the night before the service, and run by the program, point by point, minute by minute the next morning in church. On the top of the hour, "the one-hour dry cleaning service," still leaves you dry in the Spirit, or the "about an hour Lenscrafters deal" still leaves you blind in the things of the Spirit.

How God despises this humanistic man-made "churcheology," of the modern-day so-called "Holy Ghost" church. How superficial it all has become! We like to claim that the conducting of the regular church service is neither by might, nor by power, but we still refuse to give the Holy Spirit the control of the service. We pray religiously and say that the Holy Spirit is in charge of the service, but then we promise to finish the PROGRAM in exactly 60 minutes. Well, 60 minutes sounds more like a TV program than something that belongs in the church. In most Christian circles the Holy Spirit is totally ignored and kept away from the church doors, because both the move of the Spirit (REVIVAL) and the realization of Him as a person (HIS FELLOWSHIP AND CONTROL), are unacceptable to the modern-day church. The church community of today is SUPERFICIAL. It is nothing other than secular HU-MANISM. The deeper life of the Spirit, the everyday walk in the Spirit, our communication and conversation with the Spirit as a person and friend, as well as allowing the Holy Spirit direct influence and control over our lives, are all things of the past.

The heart of God is crying today for His people to forsake their religious programs, and return to the life of the Spirit as described to us in Galatians, chapter 5:16. The Amplified Bible says it this way: "WALK AND LIVE HABITUALLY IN THE HOLY SPIRIT, RESPONSIVE TO AND CONTROLLED BY AND GUIDED BY THE SPIRIT...." How adequately this verse summarizes the four secrets to the hamburger idea. Paul is not talking about a formula, or something to confess methodically, or a quick secret prayer that will bring results. NO! He is calling the church to enter into a LIFE-STYLE OF WALKING IN THE SPIRIT EVERYDAY! When we walk in the Spirit every day, and we begin to live our lives daily in Him habitually, we will become responsive to Him (who you hang around with, you will become familiar with). Once we have become comfortable with the Holy Spirit, and responsive to His touch upon our lives, we will spontaneously allow Him to control our lives and guide us each day in God's plan for our lives. HALLELUJAH! Right here is one of the most important messages for the church today, one we MUST HEAR in this hour, and one that we MUST PURSUE WITH AC-TION if we wish to amount to anything for God in this final hour.

The cry of the Spirit is for us to return to Him, to the words of Galatians 5:16. We must return to the life of the Spirit now; not a set of laws and rules, but a wonderful discovering of the person of the Spirit of God who desires to be our personal friend. How many services have I attended, where a visiting pastor is asked to open the meeting with prayer, asking for the Holy Spirit to fall, and the rain of God to be poured out (all the right words of power and revival are lavishly used in the prayer). But it proves to be no more than the RELIGIOUS RHETORIC of the modern-day charismatic church. After the host pastor had turned the service over to me, I would begin to invite the Holy Spirit to fall upon the people. And when He begins to oblige us with His wonderful presence, the same visiting pastor who opened the service and prayed all the right things, is the first one to disappear from the meeting, often soon followed by other visiting pastors. In moments like these, I cannot help to wonder how long God is still going to put up with religious demons controlling His church, while we despise His own presence. At times like that, I begin to long intensely for the forthcoming outpouring of God's fire upon the church, to forcefully burn up and destroy every demon of religion and all their doctrines and attitudes stashed away in our dumb religious minds. Who are we to refuse God's presence and criticize the Spirit of grace, simply because His manifestations in the service do not agree with my stupid doctrines? I believe the modern-day church has come close to blasphemy, and judgement for this horrendous behaviour will inevitably come in the near future. Where the presence of God is in manifestation, we are treading on holy ground and when you bring disgrace to God's presence, you will surely drop dead, Old Testament and New Testament alike. Remember Ananias and Sapphira. As a man and a servant of God, I humbly admonish you, my readers, do not disgrace the presence of God in the congregation of the saints. Whether you believe that laughter or falling or whatever manifestation you have a problem with, is of God or not, is irrelevant. Watch yourself, pastor or pew warmer, these are the last days, and God is going to clean house before He can present you as a glorious church, blameless in His sight. Please beware and be very careful of how you handle the very holy things of God. Judgement is going to start at the house of God, and that day is very near. Watch and pray and the Holy Spirit will show you all things, but do not disgrace the presence of God because He is holy. My God, please have mercy on us!

In this final generation, all of this "plastic Christianity," must be annihilated completely. Religion will once again be replaced by a RELATIONSHIP WITH THE SPIRIT; rituals will make room for REALITY; formats for FIRE; and hype for the HOLY ANOINTING OF GOD HIMSELF. What a glorious day that will be!

2. HOLY HOOP-E-LA

Holy hoop-e-la is the second of five cheap religious substitutes which are preventing us from meeting the Holy Spirit face to face in the Spirit realm. I love noise in our services, and we need to be excited in the expression of our praise to God. Surely we need to shout and rejoice and make a joiful noise before God. But if God's anointing does not show up in the midst of all the shouting, we need to stop, and find out why He, the Holy Spirit and His presence is not there. We need to correct the mistake immediately, and begin to worship God in Spirit and in truth, until our hearts begin to touch His heart. Then the Lord will be pleased with us, and release His anointing upon us. Instead, when the anointing does not come upon our shouting and praising, we just shout louder, jump higher, sing longer, whistle more, and do gymnastics in the aisle. The modern-day church has perfected the art of holy hoop-e-la, shouting and screaming all day long without the presence of God being present. Then at the end of the day we convince ourselves that God showed up, yet no signs and wonders were performed. We can hoop-e-la all day long, bang the instruments, and shout till we drop, yet with no anointing. If noise and sound constitute the anointing, let's get the biggest sound system in the world, and we would have it made. Rather, the satanic pop groups would really have a monopoly on the anointing then, if decibels were the answer. But it is not: Noise and boisterous sound do not constitute the anointing of the Spirit, however, when the Spirit is moving, the right kind of music; Spirit anointed music will ENHANCE the anointing. Where did we learn all the hype from without any anointing? Have we learned this practice from the prophets of Baal? No, from the world system in more recent times! All the noise, right songs, beautiful lyrics, but the Holy Spirit did not show up. Why not? Because we are going through the motions, doing what we always do. We don't really expect the glory of God to blow through the building anyway, that will disturb "OUR" meeting. But most of all we don't have church with the Holy Spirit anymore. So we "SUBSTITUTE" the genuine article with hoop-e-la. We can truly hoop-e-la until everyone is worked up enough emotionally to be convinced that it is the "ANOINT-ING," but it's just noise and emotion. Holy hoop-e-la has kept us out of the presence of God. Holy hoop-e-la is what we call the "ANOINTING." Holy hoop-e-la has become the number one counterfeit of the devil to keep us out of the real presence of God in our church services. And if we don't get into the Spirit, we get nothing at all. And if we think that we do with holy hoop-e-la, we are only deceived. Let us return to the genuine anointing of the Holy Spirit, giving Him the absolute preeminence and control in our church services. Let us cut out the holy hoop-e-la and learn how to escort the Holy Spirit into our regular church services.

3. CONFESSION TO POSSESSION

The next cheap brass-like substitute after holy hoop-e-la is the CONFESSION TO POSSESSION doctrine of the modern-day faith movement. The decade of the seventies finally exploded a long awaited and much needed move of the WORD of God around the world. The first decade of this revival, from the seventies over into the eighties, was probably as pure as

106

every move of God can be among imperfect men. But in the process of time the adverse demon spirits of religion, on their quest to "religious-ize" the move, began to take effect upon this wave of revelation, and have since caused almost as much damage to the move as the initial blessing had been. God's purpose with the word revival was to root and ground His people in the truth of His Word, and to cause them to walk in the truth daily, with strong faith. Let me say right now that I emphatically believe in the absolute integrity of God's Word, its life, power and ability to create exactly what it says. That to me is the message of the word revival, or faith revival as some incorrectly refer to it. At its time of revival, the word movement was an absolute God-send, a genuine move of God. But that is not true anymore today. You see, if the devil can't beat you, he will join you. And it is impossible for the devil to beat or defeat God's Word, so he just joined the move and slowly began to push it off balance.

So the wonderful revival of faith, in the process of time, has become a "FAITH ONLY" or "WORD ONLY MOVEMENT." It has become a modern-day "PHARISEE MOVEMENT," where every jot and tittle of the Scripture is examined and scrutinized tirelessly, but the Holy Spirit Himself is totally forgotten and neglected, and the moving of the Holy Spirit totally resisted. Let me be fair to positively exclude the leader of the word movement from the pharisee movement, since this beautiful man of God, being sensitive to the Holy Spirit, has continued to move on into the move of the Holy Spirit, with joy, laughter, and gifts of the Spirit accompanying. But for the rest, or at least the majority of the faith preachers, the words of the Apostle Paul in 2 Corinthians 3:6 have come true. The move of faith has become a letter with no life, no power, no manifestations, no miracles and no flow of the Holy Spirit. It has sadly become a letter that kills, and there is no Spirit or anointing left to give life to it. To them, the

Christian walk has become a method of formulas to be confessed everyday. And if you confess it, you will have it because the Word "ONLY" is required and will get the job done. In believing this way we might as well tear John, chapters 14-16, out of our Bibles, and deny the existence of the wonderful Person of the Holy Spirit in the earth. I thank God sincerely for the truth of the Word of God which I have learned from the faith people, but I also thank God every day for the person of the Holy Spirit, for revealing Himself to me. The Holy Spirit is indeed that very precious person that Kathryn Kuhlman spoke about so intimately. The Holy Spirit wishes to become the friend of every Christian who desires His friendship and touch continually. But the Word without the Spirit is a letter that kills and it is slaying the people of the word movement without regard for anyone. The confession-brings-possession message is only a half-truth, and it has steered people away from the Person of the Holy Spirit. Instead of people seeking the Spirit, endeavouring to hear His voice through times of intimacy in His presence, and seek His guidance, they just keep confessing the Word like a gramophone that got stuck on the same old tune without ever lending a listening ear to the voice of the Holy Spirit inside them. It is the Word of God that is found in the Scripture, not the voice of God. The Holy Spirit is the only Person in the Godhead on earth, and if we desire PERSONAL contact with God and hear His voice, we must find the Holy Spirit in prayer and fellowship.

Personal guidance for my own individual life does not come through the Word of God, because God's Word does not say, "Gabriel, go to America and preach the Word there." There is no such Scripture in the Word. I have found my name in there, yet no "INSTRUCTIONS TO ME PERSONALLY!" But Jesus said in John 14-16 that the Holy Spirit will become our guide (John 16:13). The Word of God is the giver of revelation knowledge.

The Holy Spirit is the revealer of my destiny, telling me what God wants me to do with that word knowledge. He is my "GUIDE." God's Word tells me "HOW" to live. The Holy Spirit tells me "WHAT" to do with my life in Christ. And if we do not develop this wonderful intimate relationship with the Person of the Holy Spirit, we forfeit God's personal plan with our individual lives. In most instances, confession brings spiritual recession, and not possession. The formulas of modern-day Christianity must make room for friendship and fellowship with the wonderful Person of the Holy Spirit.

4. THE JESUS SYNDROME

The next cheap spiritual substitute taking the place of the Holy Spirit in the church is what I call the "JESUS SYNDROME." It goes hand in hand with the previous point. The church has not yet realized that the Lord Jesus in "PERSON" has left the earth, and has returned to the Father in heaven, and that the Holy Spirit in "PERSON" has actually come to earth to take Jesus' place, until He returns. Christians try to reach God in Person all the time, by calling out to Jesus. When they desire to have a conversation with the Lord, they call "JESUS!" But Jesus in Person is not here on earth. Certainly, Jesus hears them, and carries their petitions to the Father; but He is no longer on earth "IN PERSON" to have personal fellowship with us. He has sent the Holy Spirit to take His place and provide us with all the personal things that we may need. Everything that God does in the earth is done on the basis of the Word, and manifested by the Person of the Holy Spirit. The Holy Spirit is the action man. The Word REVEALS it and the Spirit PERFORMS it. In the beginning it was the Holy Spirit who hovered upon the waters, waiting for the Word to begin the work of the creation. When it was all said and done, the Holy Spirit had personally created and fashioned the entire earthly creation with His hands, on behalf of the Father and

Jesus in heaven. The Holy Spirit was the actual WORKER of the will of God. This same wonderful Holy Spirit is still in the earth today, yet in the church we pay very little attention to the Person of the Holy Spirit. We usually try to maintain fellowship with Jesus in Person, even though He is not here in Person. But the Holy Spirit is! And so, all the wonderful things that Jesus said the Holy Spirit would do for us, as recorded in John, chapters 14-16, cannot be done because we are talking to the wrong person! We are talking to a Person, who has already been absent from the earth for almost 2000 years. Now, do you think the church is going to change and start talking to the Holy Spirit in PERSON? OH NO! The Jesus syndrome has bound the church for so long, and has such a powerful stronghold upon the MINDS of Christians, that it is very hard for them to start fellowshipping with the Holy Spirit in Person, and besides, we don't really talk to the Holy Spirit, unless we want to see some power. It is only then that we call upon the Holy Spirit. But God wants the church to enter into the long forgotten relationship with the person of His Spirit, because He is Jesus' "SUBSTITUTE" on earth until the Lord Jesus Himself returns.

5. THE SPIRIT OF RELIGION

The spirit of religion itself is a very dangerous cheap substitute in the house of God, and has probably been the most powerful and successful enemy of the church over the last 2000 years. The spirit of religion promotes SPIRITUAL RITUALS which have a FORM of godliness, but no power or anointing to them. The list of religious rituals is never ending, from candlelight vigils; to burning "holy incense"; to reading prayers from books aloud, to kneeling before altars without repentance; to confession cubicles and the list goes on and on! From people sitting in the same chair in church every Sunday; to singing the same songs; to prophesying after the third hymn is sung, etc. Shall I go on with the list of favourite things that we like to do habitually in church every Sunday morning? They are rituals without any power. Religious spirits steal away truth and power from the church. The first half of the 20th century, in the church distinguished itself as a period of great POWER (1900-1957). The latter part of the 20th century, on the other hand, has seen a tremendous restoration of TRUTH in the church, yet the true anointing and power of the church has greatly declined since the late fifties. It is therefore fair to say that the church today possesses far less of the power of God in operation than the Pentecostal church at the beginning of the 20th century. Power is restored to the church through the Holy Spirit; so prepare yourself for a great move of the Spirit in these days that are to follow.

Religion is Satan's idea of a defeated Christianity. Religion is like an orange squeezer. It will squeeze all the life out of you and leave you dry, spent and power-less. Religion allows no freedom, spontaneity, noise, expression or liberty towards God. It binds people to a rigid PROGRAM with no accommodation or provision made for the moving of the Holy Spirit, nor the manifestation of His gifts. But all of this is soon to change. The fire of the Holy Spirit will soon start to reckon with every opposing force that has troubled the church for so many years! Religious devils and all their religious doctrines will soon be banned from the church, allowing the Spirit of God to take up His rightful place in our midst.

HEARING THE VOICE OF GOD

All of these cheap religious substitutes have contributed to the inability of the present-day church to hear the voice of God personally, person after person. But as we move back over into the Spirit, our newfound relationship with the Holy Spirit will soon open up some vast new territories in the Spirit realm to us. Part of these newfound territories is the ability to hear and distinguish the voice of the Holy Spirit, as He leads us into adventures and experiences in the realms of God, never experienced before. One of these new experiences is the impartation of "WITTY INVENTIONS," as described in the Word of God. The impartation of a witty invention by the Holy Spirit to a believer will instill the ability and the knowledge in the heart of the person involved to create, manufacture, or produce some new invention in society. This new or modern invention will be able to provide a practical answer, or fill the need concerning a pressing requirement in the secular world, where the need for this new invention is absolutely great and overwhelming. When the idea of the witty invention is put into production, it will drastically change society, and also earn its OWNER millions, if not billions of dollars for himself and for the kingdom of God. The message of this chapter demands a compliance with the aforementioned four hamburger secrets which hold the keys to the hamburger idea.

Discovering the person of the Holy Spirit; establishing a relationship with Him in person; developing a friendship and closeness in that relationship; and responding to His instructions with corresponding action when He speaks to you the four hamburger secrets which will bring the miracle of the hamburger idea into reality in our lives! God is calling His people to return to a habitual spontaneous joy-filled adventure of WALKING IN THE HOLY SPIRIT everyday. The four hamburger secrets will open the way to the hamburger idea.

WITTY INVENTIONS

"I wisdom dwell with prudence, and find out KNOWLEDGE OF WITTY INVENTIONS" (Prov. 8:12,

KJV). WITTY INVENTIONS! That means ingenious discoveries, or the modern-day phenomena of the advancement of technology in society! New discoveries! The 20th century has seen the discovery and exploration of modern inventions such as never before in the history of man. The last 95 years have produced more discoveries in technology than the total 5900 years of human existence prior to this century. And still the discovering of modern inventions in the earth are as unlimited as God is, because every creative idea of the universe originates in God. He is the chief architect, creator, and inventor of everything in the universe, including our little planet. Our God is the sole inspiration and giver of all WITTY INVENTIONS represented in the earth today. The advancement of technology and science and all their modern-day achievements have their source in God, and were directly imparted to man by the Holy Spirit. The spectacular increased advancement and development of technology in our day is the gift of God to a progressive society, all according to His plan. The prophet Daniel prophesied of old that knowledge will increase at the time of the end (Dan. 12:4), and the 20th century has certainly been a time of rapid and supernatural expansion of knowledge in our planet.

How close we have come to the end of this age. From the fourth century until the beginning of the twentieth century, it required no less than 1500 years for mankind to double the knowledge of our earth one time. From 1900 until 1950 the process was repeated, but the second time it only took 50 years to double our earthly knowledge again. But this progression of knowledge is really on the increase after 1950. From 1950 until 1965 the process was repeated again in only 15 years. It took only one decade to double all our knowledge again from 1965 to 1975, only ten years! Yet in the decade of the eighties it is even more shocking. During this decade our knowledge of the earth was duplicated every 3.5 years, repeating the entire process three times in one decade only. Now in the decade of the nineties, the truth is almost unbelievable. The knowledge of man on earth is now being doubled every six to seven months, a staggering phenomena of modern time. This present rate of growth in technology, far exceeds the wildest dreams and expectations of any previous generation. The problem with this incredible phenomenon is that manufacturers cannot keep up with the rapid changes of technology. As soon as the new product is introduced to society, the new improved version is already patterned and on its way to the outlets not long after, which will then render the latest product on the shelves obsolete. We are witnessing the fulfillment of Daniel's prophecy before our eyes.

WITTY INVENTIONS of God come through the voice of the Holy Spirit, speaking such revelation to us. It can also be given to us through visions, dreams or even an angel sent to us from God. As is the case with divine guidance, these witty inventions usually come primarily through the voice of the Holy Spirit. It is like a calling of God upon our lives financially. This calling is irrevocable and unchangeable. When we accept it, it becomes a vision in our lives. When we pursue the vision it becomes a "GOAL." As we pursue that goal, we find and develop our "MINISTRY." When we fulfill the ministry in due course, we reap the blessing of the Lord.

Let's summarize it as follows:

THE CALLING (irrevocable, unchangeable).

THE VISION or PLAN for our lives. (When we accept and pursue the calling.)

THE GOAL or PURPOSE for our lives. (The thing that we focus upon or aim at.)

THE MINISTRY (STEWARDSHIP). (When we fulfill it, it produces FRUIT.)

THE REWARD. (The blessing that God bestows upon us for our faithfulness.)

114

Let's observe it in the following manner:

THE CALLING: What God wants me to do.

THE VISION: What we set out to do.

THE GOAL: What we will eventually accomplish (if we hold on to the end).

THE MINISTRY: God's way for you to serve Him on earth, through His calling upon your life professionally.

THE REWARD: God's eternal response to your faithfulness to the call, here on earth as well as throughout eternity.

OBSTRUCTION

The general atmosphere and mind-set of the average Christian at large is still a major obstacle to the discovery of witty innovations for the following reasons:

1. THE POVERTY AND FALSE HUMILITY LIFE-STYLE OF THE CHURCH

The poverty doctrines and the false "worm-like" attitude of unworthiness has destroyed innovativeness among Christians. People with an unworthy self-image do not become explorers, entrepreneurs or pioneers in the development of society. Instead of being on the cutting edge of the development of society, the church has taken a back seat to the modernization of society.

2. THE INTELLECTUALISM OF THE CHURCH

The present-day church has become too clever for God. We are going to figure out everything in our heads, because we are intelligent enough. So we just use our brains. The problem is that the creativity of God does not flow out of brain matter, but out of the human spirit as inspired by the Holy Spirit. The four hamburger secrets on the contrary, is the way to go!

3. THE JESUS SYNDROME

The incorrect assumption that Jesus is still on the earth, and that He can be contacted for personal ministry, instead of the Holy Spirit, has separated the church from hearing the voice of God. The Holy Spirit is the person in the godhead who will speak to us the words which He hears from Jesus and the Father (John 16:13-15). Once again the four hamburger secrets are the way out of this dilemma.

4. THE TUNNEL VISION LIFE-STYLE OF CHRISTIANS

Tunnel vision Christianity causes God's people to be so overwhelmed by their own personal needs in their own little world, that they fail to see and appreciate the universal plan of God for the church today. Instead of having a pioneering spirit, looking for new opportunities and ideas, Christians at large have maintained a settler's spirit, camping and settling just where they are forever. With the tent pins firmly anchored to the ground, no progress or change is at all possible. The future will simply pass you by.

5. PROPHETIC IGNORANCE

So many Christians today just do not realize the urgency of this hour, and that it is indeed the final hour of the church on the earth, and that God has an enormous prophetic plan of great glory and victory for the church. This plan includes the aggressive reaping of an end-time harvest of literally billions of souls by the church. Many Christians have the attitude that they are trying to hold on till the end, barely making it from day to day, instead of MAKING HISTORY AND MAKING A DIFFERENCE FOR THE FUTURE.

A troublesome situation nevertheless has occurred along with the rapid expansion of science and technology during the 20th century. The Lord Jesus Christ has restored the spirit of dominion back to the church as explained above, yet in spite of this fact, modern-day inventors of society, or the people who are actually responsible for fulfilling Daniel's prophecy are at large nonbelievers, and some are even atheist. What a tragedy! Unbelievers were primarily responsible for the explosion of technology during the 20th century. Daniel's prophecy is being carried out and fulfilled by the heathen, not the people of God. What a disturbing fact this is! The born-again church, indwelled by the Spirit of God with all the potential of heavens creativity inside our spirit-man, is not fulfilling the prophecy of the Scripture. This unpleasant situation used to trouble me years ago until I found out the reason for this lopsided reality.

MODERN-DAY TECHNOLOGY

We need to understand that ALL the prophetic utterances of God's Word are destined to be fulfilled in these last days, not just some of them. The church is guilty of selecting only some of the end-time prophecies to teach and explain to the body of Christ. Whatever prophecies suit our doctrines are the ones which we select, popularize and teach. But in the process, we leave out most of the total package of end-time prophecies. The most popular offhand are the ones concerning Israel. And of course they are important and biblically legitimate, and we should always teach them without compromise or hesitation. But on the other hand, what about all the prophecies concerning the church of the latter days? The church is equally important concerning its position in end-time prophecy. I have found no less than 50 miraculous end-time Bible prophecies regarding the church. Each one of these prophecies are powerful enough to unleash a global revival of Christianity, and together they will cause an explosion of glory to take place on the earth before the Lord's return. I am sure that there are more than the 50 that I have found. Whether your favorite end-time doctrine is Israel; the rapture of the church; the great tribulation; the Battle of Armageddon, or whatever else, we must learn to abide by the golden rules which govern all end-time predictive prophecy stated here as follows:

1.   All end-time prophecy concerning Israel, the church, and the heathen empires of the wicked are bound to be fulfilled.

2.   Every end-time prophecy is destined to be fulfilled at its individually appointed time, as ordained by God.

3.   All three categories of end-time prophecy (Israel, the church, and the heathen) are presently being fulfilled side by side.

4.   The end-time prophecies concerning the church will finish their course FIRST, close out the church age and allow the church to be raptured to heaven. Since the church will be first in the fulfilling of her series of end-time prophecies, we should actually watch the church even closer than Israel. We should simply focus on end-time prophecies concerning the church more than the prophecies regarding the other two categories, namely Israel and the heathen.

The church should therefore of necessity take the lead in our quest for rounding up all the end-time prophecies. But God's people for some reason or other are not instrumental in the fulfillment of end-time prophecies, and are presently lagging behind. The shocking fact of the matter is that God will utilize the heathen to a point, using them limitedly and temporarily to fulfill prophecies that are coming up for fulfillment, while the church is still asleep. Even though the Lord prefers to work through the church, His second choice will be to utilize the unbeliever to fulfill His plan. God's Word fully supports this fact with examples such as King Pharaoh during Joseph's time, and King Nebuchadnezzar during the time of Daniel in Babylon, and many others. The church during the 20th century has been vehemently opposed to the modern-day development of technology; fighting against every new invention of society, trying very hard to get it banned before it gains a foothold and becomes popular. These are the work of spirits of TRADITION, who never want CHANGE, and will ALWAYS resist change. They lose their effectiveness and power when things change. They are like a familiar spirit of the environment. When the environment changes, they lose their influence and power. Things have to remain constant and always the same, in order for these spirits to remain effective. Spirits of tradition that work in the church, have resisted the advancement of modern-day technology, because they hate the changes that new technology would produce.

Here are some significant examples of new technology that spirits of tradition in the church have vehemently resisted.

CHURCH RESISTANCE

The invention of the automobile at the turn of the century was immediately condemned by the church as evil, yet as soon as the model-T Ford became more affordable, every Christian was standing in line to purchase one. Today, life without the automobile is unthinkable. Preachers today thank God for cars and interstate highways as a tool for us to fulfill our ministries. What about the radio? It was condemned by the church as a propaganda medium for the devil for a number of years, before we ever began to see its value as a communications medium for the Gospel. The poor television was fiercely condemned by the church as the one-eye monster or the devil's eye, a messenger sent from hell. There are many Christians today who are still opposed to the television and will not have one in their homes, but they will come over to your home and watch the super bowl on the small screen on super bowl Sunday. What hypocrisy! But, thank God others in the church have been able to recognize the television as probably the most powerful communications medium made available to the church for the spreading of the Gospel during the 20th century. Through satellite television, the Gospel can and will be preached to the entire world before Jesus returns. If it had not been for the religious shortsightedness of church leaders in the 1940's, many of the television rights which were literally given away by the U.S. government in those days, would have fallen in the hands of the church. However, only the secular media was interested in television in those days, and the church community once again lost out. Those inexpensive television rights made available so reasonably in the early days of television, cost a fortune today.

During the decade of the seventies, many prophetic books flooded the market opposing the computerizations of the coming society, because of its seemingly forerunner status for the antichrist, linking it to the implementation of the 666 number of the antichrist in the future. Store scanners, grocery labels, automated tellers, and computers were all severely condemned at first. Has it ever crossed our minds in the church world, that we are opposing the plans of God and the advancement of knowledge according to the Word of God as prophesied of old through the prophet Daniel? (Dan. 12:4). The fear-filled warped end-time message of horror, preached by the church for so long, is responsible for this defeated attitude of misery and death. We are afraid of all new technology, because the antichrist will get a hold of it and destroy people with it. It has only been very recently that the church has begun to read the end of the BOOK to find out that we, the church, will triumph over evil, and that the antichrist cannot even be revealed until the church has departed from the scene, much less pose a threat to anybody on earth while the church is still on this planet. There are many Christians still today who don't know this truth. They want to build underground shelters and hide away from the antichrist. Meanwhile, the antichrist is hiding away from the church in this final generation, waiting anxiously for our subsequent departure!

As we can see in the event of the automobile, radio, television, computers, and a host of other modern inventions of our time, God intends for us to have and use these modern inventions as tools for preaching the Gospel. This entire book for instance has been typed out on a computer, the information was then transferred to a computer disk, whereafter it was sent to the printer to prepare it for printing. Let's use the technology for the benefit of spreading the Gospel. There is still a great world harvest to reap in our generation, and we will need every tool available to get the job done. Thank God for Christian radio, Christian television, and every other modern tool in the assistance of the spreading of the Gospel. When we wake up to reality, we will change our attitude about the modern inventions of society. Perhaps then, we will begin to avail ourselves to the Holy Spirit, so that He may use us to produce the coming discoveries in technology and science, instead of God having to use an unbeliever, due to the religiously old-fashioned outdated viewpoint of the church.

HOLY SPIRIT PARTNERSHIP

I believe that if God's people were in tune with the Holy Spirit in days gone by, and were listening to His voice, that God would have used many Christians in this age of technology to invent and discover some of the modern technologies of our century. This would have carried a twofold blessing. First, these Christians would have been accredited by God for helping to fulfill the prophecy of Daniel concerning the advancement of knowledge and its subsequent implementation, and second, they would have obtained great wealth through their work, a wealth placed at the disposal of the church for the spreading of the Gospel in these last days. But it is not too late yet. God is still looking for people who would be willing to become partners with Him in the advancement of technology through witty inventions, and their subsequent sponsoring of the Gospel in this crucial hour. I believe this truth to be the "DESTINY" of many Christians in these last days. Let's begin to seek the Holy Spirit for God's plan in this hour.

SECRET DISCOVERY

For several years of my young life I resisted the call of God upon my life to enter the ministry. Instead of becoming a preacher, I used to pray and ask God to give me a ministry of giving. The compassion of God in my heart, and the experience of growing up in poverty caused me to seek a ministry of giving from the Lord, so that I could help to destroy the pain of poverty in people's lives. I used to weep many a night in prayer, trying to persuade the Lord to grant me my desire. But He would not. (I am still so sensitive to the horrors of poverty that I begin to cry very easily at the sight of poverty and human oppression.) I hate poverty so intensely, that there are not enough words to express my hatred. When TV commercials begin to show the suffering children of Africa or South America, it tears me up and I hasten away from the television weeping, not able to look at their suffering. My wife and I are presently supporting a number of those poor starving children. I wish I could feed everyone of them every day, and have a house big enough to bring them into, and let them all sit on my lap every night. I wish that I could wipe away their tears, hold them in my arms, and love them all, and tell them that they are valuable and precious to Jesus.

But God would not allow me to become a businessman. I took a lot of time and effort to try to persuade Him to change His mind, but He would not. I never asked to be a minister and preach the Gospel. I did not really want to preach at first. But it was during the times of beseeching Him for great riches and wealth that I made a secret discovery. Through all my arguments with the Holy Spirit, I discovered the secret of what I term "GOD'S HOLY GHOST HAMBURGER IDEA." I used to say to the Holy Spirit, "Show me the secret of a new invention of something that will be so precious to society that it will be sought after by millions of people; a design of something as revolutionary as the automobile or the airplane. Help me to discover some mineral in the earth that would become more precious than gold, or help me to invent something more spectacular and more revolutionary to technology than computers. Give me a CREATIVE IDEA, precious Holy Spirit. You are the creative one of God." These are the kind of conversations which I used to have with the Holy Spirit. Then the day came that changed my life forever. It was the day when the Holy Spirit spoke up clearly in my spirit and commanded me not to pray this kind of prayer anymore. Instead of being distressed by His sudden refusal of my persistent request, I realized what had happened and I became overly excited. The Holy Spirit did not want me to pray this way anymore, because, as a full-time minister of the Gospel, I did not qualify for creative business ventures. Yet I understood that day, that without any doubt, I had found the SECRET WHICH WILL UNLOCK AND RELEASE THE CREATIVE ABILITY OF GOD in people's lives. The Holy Spirit then told me that I should not continue with this request any longer because it contradicts God's plan for my life. It was not in His plan for me to produce witty inventions. It was not meant for me to enter the creative realm of inventions in God for the advancement of technology and the financial support of the Gospel. I immediately understood what the Holy Spirit was telling me. And I accepted it immediately. But it had changed my life forever. I realized that I had tapped into the UNLIMITED INNOVATIVE RESOURCES of God with my continual seeking after wealth for God's kingdom. Even though I was refused the opportunity to enter the creative realms of God in business, there are many Christians worldwide who will have the opportunity to actually enter into this place with God, providing that His plan for their lives did not contradict it, as was the case with mine.

THE HOLY GHOST HAMBURGER IDEA

The secret which I had discovered through fellowship with the Holy Spirit that day is the secret which I have entitled: "God's Holy Ghost hamburger idea." The hamburger is probably the most vivid and comprehensive exponent of the creativity of the Holy Spirit communicated to man. Someone (through the Holy Spirit, I'm sure) got ahold of a very simple idea: to take a flat piece of meat, slap two bread buns on both ends, stuff some salad and lettuce in-between, along with some mayonnaise or mustard, and call it "A HAMBURGER." It was a simple concept to provide a quick inexpensive meal in order to supply the workforce with an adequate lunch, to still the hunger temporarily, and tie them over until dinnertime. The success of the hamburger has been astronomical. The simple hamburger has made millions and millions of dollars all over the world, and this is only the beginning of its great success. The hamburger has found a place in the hearts of many nations, and is a conquerer of nations in the true sense of the word. Even in Moscow (Russia), in the heart of the former Soviet communist state, the illustrious hamburger has conquered the hearts of people. The incredible success of the hamburger can be attributed to the following five things:

1. The hamburger is easy to make or produce.

2. The hamburger is very inexpensive to produce.

3. The hamburger can be afforded by everyone on the street.

4. The hamburger is needed by everyone; its market is the world.

5. The hamburger will be purchased by all people worldwide repeatedly, again and again. The need for the hamburger brings only temporary satisfaction. When the need reappears, the hamburger is purchased again. The market for the hamburger is inexhaustible. What a winner!

I believe the Holy Spirit is waiting for Christians to seek Him concerning "A HAMBURGER IDEA" for this hour. By this I mean a similar discovery or invention with all five above mentioned secrets to success. God can show you an innovative idea of something not yet known to man. It could be something very advanced in technology, or something that is based upon a very simple concept, plain and simple, yet as powerful and productive as the hamburger. The day and the hour has come for the body of Christ to pursue the Holy Spirit, so that He may give you an idea of something that you can use and develop, to produce incredible success, and bless the body of Christ with in these last days. Not everyone can be an "EINSTEIN" but many of us can handle something as simple yet revolutionary as a hamburger. God is no respecter of persons. If you volunteer, and seek the Lord for an innovative idea, and pursue the Holy Spirit through the four hamburger secrets, so that you may be blessed and be able to make lots of money for God's kingdom in these days of glory, the Holy Spirit will oblige you. Let me remind you of what Jesus said when He preached in His home town of Nazareth. He said that there were many widows in Israel in the days of ELIJAH the prophet, during that severe famine, but Elijah was sent only to the poor widow of Zarephath. And there were many lepers in Israel during the time of Naaman, yet none of them were cleansed but Naaman the Syrian. Even so, if you take this message to heart and beseech the Holy Spirit to give you a Holy Ghost hamburger idea, God will accommodate you and use you mightily to bless His kingdom financially in these last days. Whether you are a mighty man like Naaman the Syrian, or an ordinary poor widow like the widow of Zarephath. It makes no difference to God. He will bless you mightily, and use you creatively.

Here is a ministry that I personally desired to have and sought diligently. But it was not to be. My part in God's Holy Ghost hamburger idea is to share this secret with you, and show you how you can find the heart of God concerning the unlimited resources of God's creativity for yourself. I challenge you to find God's Holy Ghost hamburger idea for your life, and to seek God for the very unique plan of prosperity which He has prepared for you. Please, begin to implement the four secrets of the hamburger idea today. Incorporate these secrets into your daily life. Pursue the Holy Spirit from this day on, seek Him out of the compassion of your heart, not with the wrong motive of greed. My prayer is that you will do this from today on, and that you will be able to find God's Holy Ghost hamburger idea for your life in the near future. A warning to you though, beware of the religious hindrances and snares of the devil. Satan will do everything in his power to prevent you from ever entering into the wonderful creativity of God. The majority of believers, who after reading this book, will qualify for this great blessing reserved especially for the end-time church. God has a unique Holy Ghost hamburger idea for you, one which He has reserved especially and uniquely JUST FOR YOU, to bless you, and enable you to fulfill the end-time purpose of God in the earth. We are co-laborers with the Lord in these last days. WHAT A PRIVILEGE AND HONOR!

6 | The Regeneration of Resources

"And [God] Who provides seed for the sower and bread for eating will also provide and multiply your [resources]...." 2 Corinthians 9:10, AMP

This book tells the story of a fivefold plan of God to restore His church financially for the end-time harvest. Each of these five ventures are supernatural occurrences. The first one is the *Blessing of God upon our labor in the last days*. Through the blessing of our handiwork, God will increase and escalate our business and careers beyond the regular growth of years of faithful hard work. We may perhaps see the progress of 20 years of blessing condensed into a two-to three-year period only. This phenomenon will surely take place, but the rate of increase is not sure, that is up to God, yet nevertheless, it will be accelerated in accordance with God's plan for every individual and the amount of time remaining before His return. The second venture is *the transferring of the wealth of the wicked to the righteous.* This prophetic event will be carried out supernaturally by the Holy Spirit at the prophetic time set by God in heaven. According to the prophetic calculations of end-time scholars, the return of Jesus could be a mere 10 to 20 years away; at the most slightly more than 20; or at the least just less than 10. So, according to Bible prophecy, the Lord will return during this present generation, which is a true biblical fact that can be proven systematically from God's Word by many experts in this field of end-time prophecy today.

The effort of this book must be seen in the light of the soon return of Jesus during this generation, and hopefully it may help to show us some of the financial miracles that God will perform around the world dur- ing this forthcoming end-time revival which must pre- cede the soon return of Jesus. The third venture, *the gold and the glory,* has already been preceded by a pre- paratory move of the Spirit since 1993. This new present-day move of God's Spirit is a joyful return of Holy Ghost inspired laughter, joy, and drunkenness in the Spirit, thus fulfilling the work of "PREPARATION" for the coming end-time revival.

When this anticipated end-time revival of fire soon explodes all around us, we will then enter into the full- ness of the gold and the glory with great speed. First the full measure of glory will subsequently produce the full measure of gold in the house of God. At such a time as that, the Holy Spirit will become "ALL IN ALL" in us, and bring us to the fourth financial venture by dishing out *"HAMBURGER IDEAS"* over the place. The creative ideas of God working through His church will transform the world as we know it, and produce bil- lions of dollars for the work of the ministry worldwide. During that time, they will say: "Can it get any better than this?" And the answer is a big "YES!"

After the first four financial blessings have conquered the world, we would not know how to contain all the wealth that we have received! But God is not done yet, the best is yet to come! Now is the time for the ultimate venture of God's outpouring of wealth for the last-day church. During the manifestation of the four miracles we've just mentioned, the emphasis was on the RESOURCE itself and how God can bless the RESOURCE. We will see God BLESS the resource, and then transfer the resource from one person to another. Then we will see God bring the RESOURCE into His presence in the house of the Lord. Last, we will then see God place the RESOURCE in the hands of individuals through creative discoveries and great wisdom. These were the first four financial ventures of God's end-time plan! Now, at this point of the end-time revival, we will see God touching the resource itself, MULTIPLYING its existence so that it *EXPLODES AND INCREASES* in growth daily before our very eyes, until the Lord of glory appears on the clouds of glory. The SOURCE will finally touch the RESOURCE with miracle power multiplying it unlimitedly, whereafter the SOURCE Himself will appear in all of His glory.

MIRACULOUS RESOURCES

"And God who provides seed for the sower and bread for eating will also provide and MULTIPLY YOUR RESOURCES for sowing and increase the fruits of your righteousness" (2 Cor. 9:10, AMP).

This final chapter will tell the story of the fifth and final event that the Lord showed me concerning His end-time financial plan for the church. It is called the *MULTIPLYING OF RESOURCES*.

This fifth event of God's financial plan is so outstanding, extraordinary, unusual and almost impossible, that the word *supernatural* hardly does any justice to it! **"MIRACULOUS"** alone would justify its description. When this outstanding and astounding miracle suddenly bursts upon the scene, God will suddenly begin to regenerate the resources of the church in a miraculous fashion, leaving the world in a complete state of shock, at the sudden display of heaven's great power. The miracle of the regeneration of our existing resources is something completely unknown to man in modern times. Only three people in the Bible were ever used of God to perform this kind of miracle, and the last one was none less than the Lord Jesus Himself during His earthly ministry. As we take a closer look, we will notice that this miracle of old was prophesied to reoccur in the last days before the return of Jesus. As you read this chapter carefully, I trust that your heart will be thrilled along with mine at the beauty of this message, as we anticipate its soon manifestation and realization, as God miraculously brings it to life before our very eyes in the very near future.

A MIRACULOUS MOMENT

Everything about this message has been absolutely extraordinary to me, even the way in which I received it. Two of the five messages in this book were supernaturally imparted to me by the Lord. The first one was the *gold and the glory*, and the second one is this one that I am about to relate to you.

This message was given to me by the Lord while ministering in a church in Alabama on 29 September, 1995, at an evening service. During the altar service, I felt an unusually strong anointing of God's Spirit come upon me. The rest happened quickly. I do not remember if my eyes were opened or closed. Suddenly I was able to look right on the inside of myself and saw a sheet of paper with a message written upon it. Instinctively, I read the first few lines; after a few moments my eyes began to trace down the page to observe some of the Scripture passages recorded. I was able to read these lines at an astounding pace, and within moments, I had recorded all the Scriptures on that sheet within me. After this, I endeavoured to continue reading some more information off the page, but in a flash the sheet of paper was suddenly removed from my eyes. It was like a flash of bright light, almost like a firecracker going off in the dark. Then suddenly, everything was back to normal, the vision had disappeared as fast as it had initially appeared. I no longer had a desire to see more of the vision, as the whole message was branded into my spirit when it flashed before me and suddenly disappeared. I knew then that the whole message had already been recorded within my inner man. It was quite an awesome experience. I recall the fact that immediately following the vision, tears filled my eyes at its conclusion. It was just the goodness of God. Since that wonderful experience, I have not stopped rejoicing over what we are about to see as a result of God's wonderful plans for our generation in these last days.

PROPHETIC HOUR OF THE MIRACULOUS

The miraculous works of God are vastly absent from the church today. And all for good enough reasons. Every revival of the 20th century has had its share of truly miraculous events. Incurable diseases have been instantly healed; the dead have been brought back to life; mass healings where hordes of incurable diseases were healed in an instant were the order of the day, especially in the ministry of Dr. T.L. Osborne in Africa during the decade of the fifties. The same thing was true of the ministry of Tommy Hicks in Central and South America. In many instances missing body parts would instantly reappear in or upon people's bodies, and was witnessed by many onlookers. In the U.S. a minister by the name of A.A. Allen was probably the foremost exponent of the miracle ministry. Evangelist R.W. Schambach gives us living accounts of miraculous healings that were witnessed in and through the miracle ministry of Brother Allen. One of the most outstanding miracles was the 26 creative miracles of life manifested by God in the body of a three-year-old boy during an evening crusade meeting. I have had the privilege of hearing Brother Schambach share this story personally with a group of ministers during a camp meeting in Sweden. No less than 26 absolute miracles were needed for this dying boy to survive and enable him to lead a normal life in the future. That evening in the tent meeting God formed missing body parts within and upon the little boy's body. The Lord is the potter and we are the clay, and the potter began to form feet where there were only stumps, and straightened out his malformed arms and legs and spine. Eyes were also created where there were no eyes, as well as ears as he was deaf and mute. A total of 26 miracles completed the process of life which was not done inside the womb of his mother three years before. All of this was miraculously orchestrated by the Master's hand in a matter of minutes. "WHAT A MIRACLE!"

In the ministry of Smith Wigglesworth it was reported that no less than 23 people were raised from the dead. One of them happened to be his own wife. On one occasion, he returned from a meeting and found her dead. He raised her up against the wall, and commanded her spirit to return to her body. He simply commanded her to walk, in the name of Jesus. At the third command, her spirit returned and she began to walk! What a miracle it was! This, dear people, is the realm of the miraculous, a realm not known by the church since the late nineteen-fifties.

William Branham, who as a prophet probably stood at the forefront of the healing revival of the fifties, delivered a very significant prophecy in 1956 concerning "the miraculous." He prophesied that because of the adverse response and subsequent rejection by the church in relation to that great revival of healing, a curse would rest on the church in America for 40 years. The Pentecostal churches at large had failed to embrace this revival and incorporate it into the church. This 40-year curse would mean the departure and absence of the MIRACULOUS from the church for the prophesied period. During the next 40-year generation, starting in 1956, the church would simply be void of the miraculous works of God. And sadly so. The fulfillment of this prophetic word is still seen in churches today. Even though the church has retained a flair for the supernatural, with many wonderful manifestations of God still taking place, especially regarding divine healing, the "MIRACULOUS" things of God mentioned here have been missing since then. In this present year of 1996, we are no more than 12 months away from the end of this 40-year curse regarding the miraculous. So let us, the church of the Lord Jesus Christ, get ready for the return of God's miraculous wonders soon to be performed again in the earth!

THE NEW AGE OF FIRE

God's new age of FIRE will be His answer to the devil's new-age doctrine. It is just like it was in the days of Elijah the prophet. The devil is the same devil, but God is the same God. The same case scenario. The new-age movement is like the prophets of Baal, who challenged the truth of the living God. The new agers will have to produce some signs and wonders soon.

But like the prophets of Baal, they will come up empty-handed when challenged to a dual. God, on the other hand, will answer with *FIRE*. The liquid fire of the Holy Ghost will begin to fall on masses of people all over the world, and burn the glory of God into them, sinner and saint alike. With the fire of God falling, the new-age movement will collapse, and the end-time revival of fire, fueled by the gusty wind of the Spirit, will spread the *FIRES OF REVIVAL* rapidly around the world. HALLE-LUJAH! The revival of fire will also release the miracles of God. We, the church, will call down the rain of God's blessing like Elijah. The glory of God will fill the earth, and God's miraculous deeds will be the order of the day. GET READY CHURCH, FOR GOD'S NEW AGE OF FIRE!

THE COMING OF ELIJAH

The message of the regeneration of human resources is based upon the ministry of the prophet Elijah. Many things have been said about Elijah, but we need to understand that his ministry is a perfect prophetic pro-totype of the last days. The ministry of Elijah was a ministry of "REPENTANCE," for he was responsible for turning the wicked nation of Israel back to God in one day on Mount Carmel. Elijah's ministry is supposed to be a repetitive one throughout the future, concluding at the time of the battle of Armaggeddon. By repetitive we mean that Elijah's ministry was destined by God to reoccur, to play itself out again, at different times in the future, according to God's will. This prophetic rep-etition of Elijah's ministry rests upon the truth of two reasons.

The first reason is that on earth, Elijah never com-pleted his ministry. Depressed and full of self-pity after his enormous success on Carmel, and wearied by Jezebel's death threats against his life, he wished to die. Is this not ironic though, at that point in time Elijah wished to die, yet in reality today, he is still alive in heaven? I believe the Lord saw his distress and began to grant him a release of his ministry. He sent Elijah to anoint Hazael as king over Syria; Jehu as king over Israel; and Elisha as prophet in his place. These three men, God said to Elijah, will carry out God's judgement until an end is made of all of Israel's rebellion against God during that generation. Elijah would still prophesy Ahab's death to him personally, but an opportunity to reckon with Jezebel would not occur.

It was not very long after King Ahab's death occurred, that the time had come for Elijah to be raptured to heaven. His anointing and ministry, however, did not leave with him, but was passed on to Elisha in the form of Elijah's mantle, which fell from him as he ascended to heaven. Elisha, according to his last wish to Elijah, would carry a double portion of his predecessor's anointing as a prophet. The slaughter of the servants of Baal and the ungodly enemies of Israel was to continue under Jehu, Hazael and Elisha. The evil reign of Ahab had to come to an end, and finally Jezebel would die and suffer the very same violent death that Elijah had prophesied over her. These things though would transpire during Elisha's ministry and not under Elijah's. So Elijah's ministry was never completed during his lifetime, instead God raptured him to heaven.

The second reason for the repetition of Elijah's ministry is the prophecies of the Word of God signifying a return of his ministry, even many years after the ministry of Elisha had succeeded the ministry of Elijah in the same vein. This prophetic reoccurrence of Elijah's ministry would take place not only once, but an actual total of four times, spanning thousands of years into the future, until the end of the Tribulation Period, at the battle of Armageddon!

The return of Elijah's ministry occurs no less than four times after the completion of both Elijah's first ministry, and his immediate follow-up ministry through the prophet Elisha. Remember now that the ministry of Elisha was both a doubling of the anointing of Elijah's ministry, as well as a continuance of the same anointing in ministry. The total ministry of Elijah therefore numbers five. The first one was the early ministry of Elijah himself, during the days of King Ahab, and the other four are all returns of the ministry of Elijah, thereafter. Here are the four reoccurring ministries of the prophet Elijah as follows:

1. JOHN THE BAPTIST

The first return or reoccurrence of the ministry of Elijah was not in the person of Elijah but by means of the same calling and anointing of Elijah which was given to John the Baptist. Luke 1:17 says that John the Baptist will go before Jesus (as His forerunner), in the "SPIRIT AND POWER OF ELIJAH." John the Baptist was anointed with a similar calling as Elijah, with the same MISSION, MESSAGE, and MINISTRY. The Elijah type of ministry through John the Baptist would serve the purpose of a FORERUNNER MINISTRY for the Lord Jesus. As the prophetic forerunner for the Lord, John's ministry would accomplish the work by doing the following six things:

A.   He will turn many of the children of Israel to the Lord, which is to have a ministry of repentance (Luke 1:16).

B.   He will go before Jesus as His forerunner (Luke 1:17). He will prepare the way for the Lord and His ministry.

C. John's forerunner ministry will be a ministry of the same spirit or anointing as of Elijah (fire and repentance).

D. John will turn the hearts of the fathers to the children (Luke 1:17). Repentance again.

E. He will turn the hearts of the disobedient to the just (Luke 1:17). Repentance again.

F. He will prepare a people for the Lord (Luke 1:17). This ministry is a sixfold ministry of repentance and change!

2. THE MOUNT OF TRANSFIGURATION

The second repetition of Elijah's ministry brings about an actual return of the person of Elijah momentarily. Elijah returns here for a brief but glorious visitation upon the Mount of Transfiguration (Matt. 17:1-8, Mark 9:2-13, Luke 9:28-36). When we examine the story and follow its explanation according to the account given to us using the gospel of Mark, we notice that the disciples began to ponder over the question of the resurrection after their supernatural encounter on the Mount of Transfiguration. Concerning this matter, the disciples proceeded to ask the Lord for the reason behind the argument of the Pharisees, since they had suggested that Elijah the prophet must come back first, before the resurrection of the dead may take place. Switching then to Matthew's account of the same story, Jesus replies by saying that Elijah WILL come first and WILL restore all things (Matt. 17:11). So Jesus is referring to a "FUTURE" appearance of Elijah. Then, in the very next verse, Jesus says something completely different concerning Elijah. Now He says that "ELIJAH HAS COME ALREADY" and that they (the Jewish authorities), did to him whatever they wished. The statement now made concerning Elijah in verse 12 is in the PAST TENSE, as opposed to the previous statement issued in verse 11, which was referring to the FUTURE.

It is clear from the two contrasting incidents of verses 11 and 12, that Jesus is speaking of two different occasions taking place at different times. Yet, nevertheless, this whole story of Elijah returning in the future, and then suddenly he has ALREADY RETURNED (all in all he has to return four times), sounds like the latest version of a back-to-the-future movie! Elijah is the man who started the "BACK TO THE FUTURE" thing. But it is really quite simple. In Matthew 17:11, Jesus agrees with Malachi and says that Elijah will return in the future before the day of judgement. But in verse 12, He is talking about a PAST appearance of Elijah. Then in verse 13, we find the answer to verse 12, or to the Elijah who has already come (past appearance). Matthew 17:13 identifies JOHN THE BAPTIST as the Elijah who has already come (PAST TENSE) as the forerunner to Jesus, to prepare the way for Him. John the Baptist is therefore the Elijah of verses 12 and 13. The question still remains as to who the Elijah of the future would be. This answer will be discussed in point four.

3. THE ELIJAH PROPHETS

The third reoccurrence of Elijah's ministry is the end-time prophetic ministry of the church prior to the rapture. As the companies of prophets during the days of Elisha, so shall a breed of end-time Elijah prophets be raised up in the church to prepare the people of God (the church), for the coming of the Lord to catch His church away. This end-time prophetic ministry will fulfill the sixfold ministry of John the Baptist (see A-F, point 1, John the Baptist). As he served as forerunner for the Lord Jesus, so these prophets will serve in a forerunner ministry to prepare both the church and the world for the ending of the dispensation of grace and the catching away of the existing church, as well as the final harvest of lost souls reaped during this final end-time revival. The Elijah prophets will prepare the way for the coming of the Lord, as John the Baptist had done in the spirit (anointing) of Elijah before Jesus' first appearance. (The continuance of the supernatural ministry and works of the Elijah prophets of the end-time church will be discussed under the "MIRACLES OF THE ELIJAH PROPHETS.")

4. ELIJAH THE FEARSOME WITNESS

The fourth and final repetition or reoccurrence of Elijah and his end-time ministry, takes place in the Book of Revelation during the great tribulation, or the second and final 3.5 years of the seven-year tribulation period. Here Elijah appears in person to prepare the way for the Second Coming of Jesus (Mal. 4:5). In Matthew 17:12, the Elijah spoken of was John the Baptist, preparing the way for Jesus' FIRST coming! In Matthew 17:11 it's Elijah himself in person, who appears to prepare the way for Jesus' SECOND coming! This description is given to us in Revelation 11:2-12. Please open your Bible and read along with me, as the passage is too lengthy to quote. Beginning in Revelation 11:2, the duration of the ministry of the two witnesses is given as 42 months, or 3.5 years. The next verse (verse 3) confirms the fact that the seven-year tribulation period will be measured in Jewish or solar-lunar years and not in modern-day calendar years, since the 42 months of verse two are now measured in actual days. The number is 42 months multiplied by 30 days per month; which is 42 x 30 = 1260 days or exactly 3.5 Jewish years (verse 2 says 42 months; 42 x 30 days = 1260 days). Verse 3 actually dispels all doubt regarding the exact period of days, since the precise number of the days is given to us as 1260 days.

When we take a closer look at this passage of Scripture, we find a sevenfold connection between the ministry of Elijah, and the future ministry of the two witnesses. When we consider these seven facts separately, they do not seem to say much to us. But when we compare them all together with Elijah's ministry, they tell an amazing story. In this particular passage of Scripture, seven characteristics of the future ministry of the two witnesses are explained to us. God's motive for revealing the ministry of the future witnesses is so that we may be able to identify them in Scripture. Many people have speculated over the identity of the two witnesses, and some even say that it is impossible to know who the two witnesses will be. But as we begin to combine Scripture together, and line up the ministry of the two witnesses with other ministries in God's Word, and with the prophecies for the last days, the identities of the two witnesses fit the description like the proverbial piece of the puzzle. Prophetically, Elijah has been prophesied to return before the great battle of Armageddon, and because Elijah had never died on the earth, but was raptured to heaven in bodily form, gives us enough ground to take Elijah as an example, and see if his ministry corresponds with all the seven characteristics of the ministry of the two witnesses. It is a PERFECT MATCH! But why do you not decide that for yourself after reading the comparison between the ministry of Elijah, and the future ministry of the two witnesses?

THE PERFECT MATCH

As we compare Elijah's ministry with that of the two witnesses of the Book of Revelation, we find that every duty of the future witnesses corresponds with the works of Elijah during his earthly ministry.

142

The FIRST CORRESPONDING FACT between Elijah and the future witnesses is that Elijah shut up the heavens for 3.5 years during the days of the prophecy of drought. Elijah said to Ahab that according to his word there shall be no dew nor rain during those years (1 Kings 17:1). The exact duration of the prophecy is confirmed by the Lord Jesus in Luke 4:25 where He says that the heavens were shut up for 3.5 years by the prophet Elijah. The 3.5 years is the exact duration of the ministry of the two witnesses, that being exactly 1260 days. The 3.5-year duration of drought, and the 3.5-year end-time ministry of Elijah, is the first corresponding point of ministry here. Looking to the second corresponding fact will meaningfully explain the 3.5 years point, concerning Elijah and the two witnesses.

The SECOND CORRESPONDING FACT between Elijah and the two witnesses is found in Revelation 11:6 where it says that the two witnesses have the power to SHUT THE HEAVENS and that there will be NO RAIN for the 3.5-year period. The first two corresponding facts of the witnesses is an exact confirmation of the previous ministry of Elijah, who also shut the heavens up so that there was no rain for 3.5 years. These two incidents of two periods of no rain for 3.5 years in the ministry of Elijah and the two witnesses are the only two incidents of this kind in the Bible, where rain is shut up in the heavens for exactly 3.5 years. *ELIJAH WILL BE INVOLVED IN BOTH INSTANCES!*

The THIRD CORRESPONDING FACT between Elijah and the two witnesses is the anointing of FIRE. The greatest victory in Elijah's ministry came upon Mount Carmel during that great and notorious display of God's power from heaven, when Elijah finally prayed for the fire to fall. God obliged, and consumed the altar as well as the sacrifice upon it with *glorious fire* from the heavens. The corresponding fact found in Revelation 11:5 says fire will proceed out of the mouths of the two witnesses when attempts are made against them to harm them in any way. Besides the fire on Mount Carmel, God also allowed fire to protect Elijah's life from the king of Israel. On one occasion, Elijah called down fire twice to consume the captain of 50 and his band of soldiers who came to arrest him. Here we see the operation of the anointing of fire to "PROTECT" Elijah. Twice a captain of 50 was sent to arrest Elijah, and twice fire was called down from heaven by Elijah to consume them. The same thing happens now in Revelation 11:5. The same anointing of fire will be seen in operation in order to protect the two witnesses from their enemies. Only this time, the fire proceeds out of the mouths of the two witnesses. However, the similarity of the usage of fire to protect the lives of the witnesses is clear, in reference to the early ministry of Elijah and is another perfect match between Elijah and the two witnesses.

The FOURTH CORRESPONDING FACT between Elijah and the two witnesses is the fact that Elijah was caught away into heaven bodily. Physically, he had never died. Physical death is the law in passing away from the earth. Every person who wants to leave this earth has to die in order to depart, and enter eternity without a physical body. God's Word says that it is appointed unto man to die "ONCE" and after that, the judgement. Of every human being who had ever lived on the earth, only two of them had never died physically. These two men had both left the earth and proceeded directly into heaven by the divine will of God. God allowed for them both to be caught away or raptured into heaven bodily. These two men are both alive now in heaven, physically, and will return as the two witnesses to be killed at the end of the 1260-day prophecy, whereafter they will be delivered from the antichrist. They are therefore the only two men who have never died on the earth, but must die after their prophecy is fulfilled (Rev. 11:7). The fact that Elijah is one of these two living witnesses still awaiting death, qualifies him as one of the two witnesses of Revelation 11. After 3.5 days of death (a day for each year of their prophecy) the two witnesses are resurrected to life again in full view of the whole world via satellite television. The corresponding fact here is the fact that Elijah had never died while on the earth, and now still has to taste death before entering eternity. Any person who has already lived and died on the earth could not qualify to be one of the two witnesses, simply because that would be re-incarnation. This fact undoubtedly narrows the field down to only two men. The forthcoming physical death of Elijah and the other witness, is the fourth corresponding fact between Elijah and the two witnesses.

The FIFTH CORRESPONDING FACT between Elijah and the two witnesses is their subsequent ascension into heaven. The corresponding fact is that Elijah, at the end of his first earthly ministry, ascended into heaven; he was caught away bodily. Now, for a second time at the completion of his second earthly ministry, Elijah is to be caught away again into heaven. History points out to us that only three men were ever raptured to heaven. The one is excluded here because He is the Lord Jesus Christ. The other two men were the only two men who had never died as seen in the previous point. Once again the facts correspond perfectly.

The SIXTH CORRESPONDING FACT between Elijah and the two witnesses is the RESURRECTION of the two witnesses after laying dead in the streets for 3.5 days, a day of death for every year of their prophecy. The power of resurrection was evidently seen in the ministry of Elijah when he raised the dead son of the widow of Zarephath to life, after his sudden passing. Elijah's ministry was one of a rare few who actually raised the dead in the days of the old covenant. The same resurrection power fell upon Elijah's successor Elisha, who also possessed the God-given ability to resurrect the dead. Elijah's own resurrection in the streets of Jerusalem is the sixth corresponding truth, identifying Elijah as one of the two witnesses of Revelation 11.

The SEVENTH CORRESPONDING FACT between Elijah and the two witnesses is the prophecy of the prophet Malachi as recorded in Malachi 4:5, which says that God will send Israel the prophet Elijah before the coming of the great and dreadful day of the Lord. This dreadful day of the Lord is the return of Jesus at the end of the seven-year tribulation period, when He returns to deliver Israel from the antichrist at the Battle of Armageddon. The last 3.5 years of the tribulation concludes at the return of Israel's Messiah, thus fulfilling the prophecy of Malachi. The return of Elijah as one of the two witnesses during the final 3.5 years of the tribulation places Elijah on earth prior to the return of Jesus for the Battle of Armageddon, thus fulfilling the prophecy of Malachi. The name of the second witness is not as clearly identified as that of Elijah. But the only person who qualifies and corresponds with all these seven things besides Elijah is Enoch. As Elijah, Enoch also had never died. Enoch was raptured bodily to heaven, like Elijah, and he shall be returned to the earth as a witness along with Elijah. Together with Elijah, they will fulfill the 3.5-year prophecy, be killed, resurrected, and caught up the second time to heaven, as described to us here in the Book of Revelation. Some people argue that the other witness besides Elijah would be the prophet Moses, because the witnesses will have the power to turn the water into blood, and to strike the earth with plagues. However, in my opinion, no other man could qualify to become the second witness, simply because Moses, or anyone other than Enoch, had actually died physically on earth, which subsequently disqualifies them to return to the earth as the other witness, and die a second time on the earth. The only other man who had never died on earth was Enoch, who is evidently our second witness.

In retrospect, all in all the ministry of Elijah occurs five times in total. Here they are listed together.

1. The earthly ministry of Elijah under King Ahab (1 Kings 18-2 Kings 2). Elijah in person.

2. The ministry of John the Baptist (the Gospels). Elijah represented.

3. Elijah's appearance and ministering to Jesus on the Mount of Transfiguration (Matt. 17, Mark 9, Luke 9). Elijah in person.

4. The end-time Elijah prophets of the church (substantiated by analogies and parallels in Scripture as well as the forerunner ministry of John the Baptist for Jesus' first coming). Elijah represented.

5. The physical return of Elijah as the fearsome witness of the great tribulation. Elijah in per- son.

Note that appearances number 1, 3, and 5 are the actual appearances of Elijah in person, a total of three times. The ministry and anointing of Elijah represented occurs two times. So we see two representations, and three appearances. The numbers two and three are counted here. This gives us the perfect biblical witness to the truth of God. In the mouth of two or three witnesses every word shall be established. Also, the first and last appearances are very similar; they both represent a very significant prophetic period of 3.5 years each. The ministry during these two 3.5-year periods are also very similar. During Elijah's first ministry under King Ahab, he shut up the heavens for 3.5 years. As the witness during the latter 3.5 years of the tribulation period, Elijah once again shuts up the heavens so that it does not rain for a period of 3.5 years. Two distinct periods of 3.5 years are noted, totalling seven years, which is equal to the entire duration of the great tribulation. The time periods of numbers 1 and 3 are therefore very significant, because they comprise of two equal periods of 3.5 years, representing the two halfs of the tribulation period together. The total period of Elijah's ministry as God's judge over Israel is therefore seven years. I do anticipate that the end-time prophetic ministry of the church will also comprise a seven-year period.

Here we see the perfect fivefold ministry of Elijah; an early ministry during the days of Ahab, and a latter ministry during the final 3.5 years of the tribulation of the last days. All in all the ministry of Elijah will appear a total of five times. The number five represents the administrations of God, the fivefold ministry of the New Testament church.

THE MIRACLES OF ELIJAH

The ministry of Elijah forms the foundation for the end-time prophetic ministry of the church. It is a ministry of great glory and power, truly a ministry of the miraculous as mentioned above. Let us consider the great anointing and miracles of the Elijah ministry: We clearly distinguish ten different miracles which occurred during the great ministry of Elijah. They are as follows:

1. The miracle to shut up the heavens so that it did not rain for three and a half years.
2. The miracle of Elijah's supernatural preservation during the drought.
3. The miracle of raising the dead to life.
4. The miracle of calling down the *FIRE OF GOD* on several occasions.
5. The miracle of bringing instant repentance to the nation of Israel.

6. The miracle of superhuman ability to outrun the chariot of Ahab.

7. The miracle of opening the heavens to pour down rain.

8. THE MIRACLE OF THE REGENERATION OF HUMAN RESOURCES.

9. The miracle of splitting the Jordan River apart to provide passage.

10. The miracle of being bodily caught away alive to heaven.

THE ELIJAH MINISTRY OF THE END-TIME CHURCH

The Elijah prophets, soon to be raised up, will fulfill the same sixfold ministry of John the Baptist (as described above under point 1, John the Baptist). These powerful God-sent prophets will effectively prepare the church for the Lord's return and deliver a comprehensive and all-encompassing end-time ministry to the body of Christ. When I experienced the "FLASH VISION" (as I prefer to refer to it), the Lord showed me five special qualifications of the Elijah prophets of the church, which will undoubtedly become their trademark in ministry, and set them apart for this final hour of God's glory in the church. Unless the following five spiritual qualifications of ministry are clearly seen in the lives of God's end-time Elijah prophets, they are not part of this company of prophets. Whatever claims they may issue, unless they manifest ALL of the fivefold fruit of the Elijah ministry, OR END-TIME PROPHETIC MINISTRY OF THE CHURCH, however credible they are as ministers in other capacities, *THEY ARE NOT PART OF THE ELIJAH PROPHETS!* Here is the fivefold end-time prophetic ministry of Elijah, to be manifested through the end-time prophets of the church.

1. GOD'S PROPHETIC END-TIME MESSAGE

These prophets will bring God's end-time prophetic Word of His specific plan of restoration for the church and revival for the world. This specific end-time revival message accurately discerned in Scripture will be their trademark. They will have the blueprint of God's end-time plan, and will deliver it to the church as God's MANDATE for this hour.

2. CALLING DOWN GOD'S FIRE

The Elijah prophets will also bring to the church the powerful message of the fire of the Holy Ghost, and will LITERALLY PRAY THE FIRE DOWN UPON PEOPLE, resulting in an explosion of revival. When they pray for the fire, it will begin to rain down in a shocking fashion. This will not be hype, emotion, or make-believe. The visible outpouring of God's fire will be witnessed by all present in the meeting place of these prophets, when they call for God's fire to fall.

3. VISIBLE SIGNS AND WONDERS

To convince people further of their mission and calling, these prophets will perform visible signs and wonders in the planets and the sun (Acts 2:17-21). They will also exercise authority over the elements of nature such as the wind, rain, clouds, and the weather. The elements of nature will obey their words. Mighty signs will be seen this way, and many people will be saved, and be delivered from Satan's kingdom and power.

4. HEALING AND MIRACLE MINISTRY

These prophets will not be showmen, but will have a pure heart after God. They will minister divine healing to many people, and perform some outstanding miracles, such as raising the dead to life before many witnesses. These miracles will bring many people to salvation in Jesus Christ, and cause people to look expectantly for the Lord's return.

5. THE REGENERATION OF HUMAN RESOURCES

By the Word of the Lord, these prophets will be able to pronounce the regeneration of people's resources in the capacity that the Lord wills at different times, and amazing miracles will happen to the astonishment of the world.

When the Elijah prophets begin to exhibit these wonderful and miraculous God-given qualities, the body of Christ will know that these prophets who are able to operate in all five of these miraculous endowments, have been anointed by God to be the end-time Elijah prophets of the church, preparing the way for the Lord's coming. Time and space will not allow us to elaborate further upon each one of these fivefold qualities of God's end-time Elijah prophets. However, I will endeavour to explain the fifth miraculous endowment of the Spirit given to them, which is also the fifth point in God's fivefold end-time plan of prosperity for the church called, "THE REGENERATION OF HUMAN RESOURCES."

A RARE MIRACLE

The miracle of the regeneration of human resources is indeed a rare one. Only three people in the history of the Bible were ever able to perform the miracle of the reproduction of earthly resources. They were Elijah (once), Elisha (twice), and the Lord Jesus Himself (five times). Jesus fed the 5000 with two loaves and five fishes, and also the crowd of 4000 on another occasion. Each time, seven baskets filled with leftovers were collected afterwards. In Luke, chapter 5, it is almost certain that Jesus performed the same kind of miracle by multiplying the fishes in the sea, enabling the disciples to report a record catch, and once again, the same miracle was performed by the Lord as recorded in John, chapter 21. The turning of the water into wine can also qualify as the same type of miracle because there was suddenly an abundance of wine flowing for everybody. As long as the waterpots were filled over and over, and wine was repeatedly poured out from them, the new wine continued to flow. So arguable, this miracle was performed no less than five times by Jesus Himself, yet it was done in a different manner each time, and under different circumstances. Its prophetic impact for today, however, justifiably takes us back to the ministry of Elijah once again, when the miracle of the multiplying of resources occurred for the first time in Bible days.

THE WIDOW OF ZAREPHATH

During the three-and-a-half-year drought in Israel according to Elijah's word, the Lord finally sent Elijah to Zarephath, after the brook Cherith had dried up. The Lord told Elijah that a widow woman would provide for him in his needs. On arrival, Elijah met her at the city gate. Immediately he proceeded to ask her for water and bread, to which she replied that she only had a handful of flour in a bin and a little oil in a jar. She went on to tell Elijah that she was gathering some sticks to make a fire and prepare a final meal for herself and her son, whereafter they will surely die (of starvation). Then in verse 13 we see the prophetic word which would miraculously multiply this poor widow's depleted resources. Elijah told her to bake him a cake FIRST, *before* she prepares it for herself and her son. Then he prophesied the miracle. "The bin of flour shall not be used up, nor shall the jar of oil run dry, until the day the Lord sends rain on the earth" (1 Kings 17:8-16). And the miracle began to happen. Incredibly, the widow's resources were regenerated every time she used them up. By reason of "USE," her little bit of flour and oil were instantly REPRODUCED supernaturally. And this astounding miracle continued to flow without fail, according to the Word of the Lord (verse 16). The prophetic word spoken by the prophet, declared that the miracle would continually reoccur, repeatedly, until after the rains had come. Of course that time is not known to us. We know that the drought lasted for three and a half years (Luke 4:25) and that Elijah was probably sustained by the ravens for approximately a year. So the miracle of multiplying the widows resources could have continued as long as two or even two and a half years. And all that time the flour and oil kept multiplying continually, even after the rain had come and the drought was finally broken. What an outstanding miracle!

ELISHA'S DOUBLE PORTION

The prophet Elisha received a double portion of Elijah's ministry upon his life. It was the same ministry, but a double portion of it and a double anointing. This double portion anointing enabled Elisha to perform the miracle of the multiplication of human resources twice as opposed to the single incident recorded in Elijah's ministry. Both instances regarding this wonderful miracle in the ministry of Elisha are found in 2 Kings, chapter 4. We find the first instance in verses 1 through 7. A certain widow of the sons of the prophets was about to lose her sons to her creditors after her husband's death. When she urgently beseeches Elisha for help, the prophet of God wanted to know what possessions she had in her home. She replied in despair that all she possessed in her household was a jar of oil. Then the prophet of God received a prophetic word for her from God. He told her to go to her neighbours, and borrow as many empty vessels as she could possibly find. Thereafter she should return to her house, shut the door behind herself and her sons, and pour the oil from the jar into all the empty vessels. As she began to pour the oil into the other containers, the most incredible miracle began to occur. One vessel after the other was filled to capacity, and the oil kept flowing constantly. Finally as the widow began to run out of empty containers, she said to her son, "Bring me another vessel." But there were no more empty vessels available. Once all the vessels were filled with the constant flowing of oil, the oil finally ceased flowing. Please note: the oil NEVER stopped flowing UNTIL all the empty containers were completely filled. What an amazing miracle! The oil would not cease from flowing as long as containers were available to pour the oil into. The big question is, "How long would this oil have continued to flow if more empty vessels would have been available?" Who knows. Probably forever! The point is though, that the supply of this wonderful miracle had become "INEXHAUSTIBLE." Truly, a miraculous multiplying and regeneration of a poor widow's resources had taken place. The abundance of filled containers, full of precious oil, was more than enough to pay the widow's debt and probably enough to secure her financially for the rest of her life on earth. What a glorious miracle! God's inexhaustible resources were released on behalf of this widow to relieve her debt, and provide for her family.

The second miracle of the multiplication of human resources in Elisha's ministry is seldom noticed. But the same kind of miracle is performed. The final three verses of chapter 4 tells the story briefly. A man from Baal-Shalisha brought 20 loaves of bread, and a little bit of grain in a sack to the company of prophets. Elisha prophetically commanded the small portion of food to be given to the prophets to eat. (Remember that Elisha was in charge of a school of prophets.) But the servant of Elisha was almost outraged at this command. The bread and grain was hardly enough for a half-dozen hungry full-grown men (these loaves were comparatively smaller compared to today's bread). But the prophet of God told his servant to feed the 100 hungry men with it anyway. As they began to eat, the bread began to multiply over and over, until all the prophets were fully satisfied, with some left over at the end. What a miracle! To feed 100 men with enough supplies for only a handful of people. The miracle had happened again, it was the second time it had occurred in the ministry of Elisha the prophet.

RESOURCES FOR THE LAST DAYS

Of the fivefold plan which the Lord had shown me concerning the financial revival of the end-time church, we have discussed the reality and impact of the first four upon society in the previous chapters. *The supernatural blessing of the works of our hands; the transference of the wealth of the wicked to the righteous; the release of the gold and the glory; and the inventions of God's Holy Ghost hamburger idea,* are four world changing and life transforming miracles that would cause a total metamorphosis of the world scene, spiritually as well as financially in these last days.

Now comes the fifth and final miracle of financial provisions for the last day church. Here God pulls out all the stops, and opens the windows of heaven and causes a flood, like the flood of Noah. It begins to rain with the rain of the Holy Spirit, until the whole earth is filled with God's glory, and the Holy Spirit has been poured out upon all flesh. Noah's rain began in the 600th year of his life, and quite possibly, the great rains of God may come in the 6000 year of the life of our earth and its establishment. God told Noah after he had completed the Ark, that seven more days will transpire before the rains would come upon the earth. Knowing that the end-time harvest would last for seven years, from the 6000th year of the planet, the great rains may last for seven more years, or seven years of harvest. The 6000th year of the planet according to the calendar is the year 2000 A.D. This might be a true indication of how long we have to wait for the flood of God's glory. But the time is short, and the work of these last days is vast, and the glory of God will be SUPER-ABUNDANT.

The multiplying of our human resources, is the ultimate blessing destined by God for the last-day church. This miracle will manifest in accordance with the examples quoted above from the ministries of Elijah and Elisha. According to the word of the Lord given to me, the end-time prophets, carrying the same anointing as Elijah, will speak this miracle into existence in all different parts of the world, and at different times, as the Spirit of God commands them to. Although these miracles occur frequently and numerously through the mouths of many prophets worldwide, it will only be done by the will and word of the Lord in every single situation. Do not think for one moment that this will erupt into a wild circus with everybody running around prophesying to everything they can lay their hands on.

At the time of the reoccurrence and reintroduction of this miracle to this final generation, God's end-time revival of fire would have already raised up the army of God's fire in the church, as explained by the prophet Joel (Joel 2:2-11). Everyone will march in his rightful place reaping the harvest and work where God has planted each soldier of His great army. At this stage of God's end-time plan in progress, the fire of God would have created a united, Holy Ghost filled and orchestrated, global force of revival in the church, and the invasion of planet earth with the Gospel of glory would be well under way. The Elijah prophets also will be spreading out all over the world, performing their five-fold end-time ministry as mentioned before, including multiplying human resources as instructed by the Lord. By then, the Holy Ghost explosion would have filled the earth with holy chaos. Evangelists will be bringing whole cities to God in a day, as in the days of Jonah in Nineveh. Apostles of the Lord will be claiming whole regions and even nations for the Lord, with the mighty moving force of the people of God following up behind them, in order to minister to the masses of people. Pastors will attempt to gather millions of people in large sport stadiums all over the world, eagerly attending to the enormous needs of their newfound flocks. Bible teachers will be gathering masses of people in smaller groups to teach them the wonderful things of God, and to prepare them for the soon return of the Lord. We are talking "REVOLUTION" now, an invasion of the forces of the church upon the whole world. The MIRACULOUS will become the norm in everything, and the harvest will come in within a few short years. This greatness of heaven's glory will complete the story of the church on earth. HALLELUJAH! The church will be perfected, and will be built together to become a Holy habitation of the Lord. The end-time harvest of God's glory will be gathered in by masses of Christians ablaze with the fire of God. The great commission will be fulfilled, all the work of the Lord through the church will be completed, and the time for the Lord's return will arrive! Our goals and visions in the Lord will be fulfilled. And the Lord will return for His church in all His splendor.

THE DEVIL'S DEFEAT

The devil and his kingdom will be in complete disarray. Having already lost control of the finances and resources of the world before this final event, the little hope that Satan might have had to regain the wealth of earth at this time will completely vanish when God begins to regenerate the resources of the church all over the world. Even if Satan could steal away all of the wealth of the church, which will never be possible again, the endless multiplication of our resources would still enable the global church to control the finances of the world right to the end, and produce God's harvest of souls successfully. The miracle of the multiplication of our resources will take place all over the world, continually, day after day; just like the woman who filled up all the empty vessels of oil. The oil did not cease to flow and multiplied continually. We are going to see the same kind of miracle occurring daily, right up to the return of the Lord.

When this type of creative miracle begins to fill the earth in these last days, and human resources are being multiplied in millions of similar situations all over the world, God's wealth will prepare the way for the return of Jesus on the clouds of glory. And the miracle of the multiplying of resources will not come to an end until the church is actually raptured to heaven. The entire world economy will be controlled by the miracle of the multiplying of earth's resources. World markets will be revolutionized each day, as the resources of wealth are multiplied everywhere from day to day. The abundant increase of earth's resources would create a new world economy daily, because the law of supply and demand would drastically increase and multiply the supplies under demand. The availability of different commodities in bulk supply, will cause the prices to fluctuate daily on the world markets. You may ask, how can stock prices ever become steady? Business people would have to take stock of the availability of every product offered on world markets everyday to determine the new price for each day. The rapid increase and multiplication of the quantities of all the merchandise will cause stocks to plummet lower and lower every day, because the rapidly increasing supply through the multiplication of resources, will cause the supply to outnumber and outperform the increasing demand everyday. The supply will increasingly outgrow the demand, causing prices to fall, day by day. Eventually, shares will be worth nothing! BUT DO NOT BE CONCERNED! We are not heading for another financial market crash.

Bear in mind now that the church is already in control of the wealth of earth. We are very rich in goods, shares, gold, money and investments. At this point, all the money withdrawn from the plummeting markets will be invested in the multiplying of human resources, so the wealth will be distributed throughout the world to meet the needs of people, and to preach the Gospel, instead of being invested in money markets! Wealth will not be hoarded up, or traded, it will be used to MEET THE NEEDS OF THE PEOPLE. Furthermore, the multiplication of the resources will take place when we DISTRIBUTE and USE the wealth to help people. In other words, it will be far better to disperse the wealth than to invest it. Remember the words of Paul in 2 Corinthians 9:10. We quoted from the amplified translation earlier. Let us consider what it says again. "And God who provides seed for the sower and bread for the eating will also provide and MULTIPLY YOUR RE-SOURCES FOR SOWING...." Yes, God will multiply our resources, but He will do it for the purpose of SOW-ING. There is no time trying to hoard up possessions and wealth. Our resources are MULTIPLIED FOR SOW-ING or GIVING. When we distribute and disperse the wealth, God will multiply it and give us the miraculous kind of return that no world market could ever offer us for an investment. Even the hundredfold return would be as nothing compared to the multiplication of resources. Here we are reminded again of the fact that it is more blessed to give than receive. As we continue to give out our wealth to the poor, and to the preaching of the Gospel around the world, what we give would liter-ally multiply and produce a flood of wealth that no interest rate could ever challenge. The multiplication of resources simply means that the more you give away, the more God will multiply back to you IMMEDIATELY! The miracle will be instantaneous! Here is just an example to explain what I am talking about: You might give away $1000 to a missionary in Africa. That $1000 would begin to multiply after you have sown it, and continue to do so everyday. The numbers would soon become staggering! Within no time the $1000 would have multiplied to a million dollars, and after that it would be a billion dollars, continuing to grow daily! It is almost frightening to imagine. But this kind of miracle knows no boundaries, limitations, or stoppages! GOD WILL MULTIPLY OUR RESOURCES FOR GIVING!

Can you imagine the impact of this great miracle upon society? When this miracle first begins to occur, hunger and starvation will probably cease in one week around the face of the globe. Poverty in the church worldwide will probably be over within the first month, and all the poverty and oppression of earth would be gone in a matter of months. There are no limitations to the explosion of this miracle all over our planet. But as part of the end-time anointing and ministry of Elijah, it is a prophetic fact, not just daydreaming. The prophetic parallels of God's Word confirms this teaching. First, there is Elijah and the double portion of Elisha, producing no less than three miracles of resources as forerunner types and symbols of the end-time ministry of the church. Second, when Israel departed from Egypt to the Promise Land, she stripped the Egyptians of all their wealth. Third, there is Noah, who gathered food and livestock in abundance of every kind before he entered into the ark. And fourth, there is the story of Joseph in Egypt, where a superabundant harvest of seven years was produced and administered by Joseph. Representing the church prophetically, all the wealth and harvest was brought to Joseph to store away. And for seven years Joseph was in control of great wealth and riches. This represents the seven years of the end-time revival and harvest. Following this seven-year period of wealth and superabundance, seven years of great famine and poverty will follow. This second seven-year period represents the seven years of the tribulation period which follows immediately after the rapture of the church, thus taking place at the end of the seven good years.

So the end-time harvest as a time of unequaled wealth is also a seven-year period of the great harvest of souls. The rapture then takes place and the tribulation period of seven years starts out with a famine (Rev. 6:5-6). Before the seven-year tribulation period is started, there is a seven-year period of harvest. This number of seven years also equals the total period of Elijah's ministry enforcing famine upon the earth, the 3.5 years during the reign of King Ahab, and the 3.5 years of the reign of the antichrist during the great tribulation. All these prophetic prototypes of God's Word substantiate the truth of this teaching. I believe the miracle of the resources to be a dominant end-time event of the church, awaiting the hour of fulfillment as soon as the fire of the Holy Spirit falls, to burst forth the spiritual revival of the last days. All of the prophetic types and shadows of glory in the Old Testament will come to pass in this latter house of glory of the church, prior to the rapture. This end-time revival will be a glorious unfolding of the prophetic types of the Old Testament in the power and great commission of the New Testament, a culmination of the two, being intensified to an astounding crescendo, peaking right at the time of the opening of the clouds for us to meet the Lord in the air.

Do You Believe?

I trust that this fivefold plan of God's end-time revolution for the church will grip your heart with joy and hope. The church has been filled with so much despair and is drifting around hopelessly without a vision. This book, however, deals exclusively with the financial aspect of the end-time revival and harvest. The glory of what God will accomplish SPIRITUALLY stretches far beyond the greatness of God's financial exploits of the end. It will take some time before we can freely proclaim that part of the revival. We have spoken about the miracles of money and the resources of the world system. If this part of the revival is difficult for people to accept, how much more will the spiritual side of this end-time revival leave people in dismay. It reminds me of the words of Jesus in John 3:12, where He speaks these words of wisdom. He says, "If I have told you earthly things and you do not believe, how will you believe if I tell you heavenly things?" If believers find it hard to believe the news of the financial revival of these last days, which concerns mostly the blessing of natural things, such as money, gold, and other precious merchandise, how will God's people believe the news of the spiritual revival and all the wonders that God will perform spiritually, during the days of the final outpouring of the Spirit upon all flesh? But thank God there are some who do believe. Some believe the prophets, and that all the Scriptures must be fulfilled, every jot and tittle thereof. But this prophetic hour, and the next one, belongs to the Master, the Lord of heaven and earth, and HIS END-TIME PROPHETIC CHURCH OF GLORY!

The ministry of Gabriel Heymans travels through-out the world to conduct end-time revival meetings and financial seminars.

To contact Gabriel Heymans for ministry engage-ments, please call our office at 904/677-4410 or our toll free number, 800/823-8820, or write to:

Gabriel Heymans Ministries
1500 Beville Road
Suite 606-256
Daytona Beach, Florida 32114

GABRIEL HEYMANS MINISTRIES

ORDER FORM — BOOKS, TAPES, VIDEOS
**NEW RELEASE

QTY.	TITLE	PRICE	TOTAL
	BOOKS		
	**The Gold & Glory of the End-Time Church	$9.95	
	TAPES		
	**Hearing the Voice of God	$25.00	
	**The Fire of God	$25.00	
	**Companionship With the Holy Spirit	$25.00	
	**Freedom From Church Religion	$45.00	
	**Church Restoration for the Final Forty Years	$45.00	
	Divine Healing Explosion	$40.00	
	Partaking of Spiritual Gifts	$12.00	
	The Gift of Exhortation	$12.00	
	Man's Return to Glory	$20.00	
	Gifts of the Holy Spirit	$28.00	
	The Force of Joy	$20.00	
	The Forthcoming Revival	$12.00	
	God's Divine Prosperity	$20.00	
	Discovering the Holy Spirit	$12.00	
	The Fresh Anointing	$28.00	
	Friendship With the Holy Spirit	$20.00	
	The Forthcoming Glory	$12.00	
	Prophecy	$20.00	
	Prophetic Events of the Last Days	$35.00	
	The Prophetic Church	$20.00	
	God's Prophetic Time Table	$35.00	
	Victory Over Deception	$20.00	
	Victory Against All Odds	$12.00	
	Campmeeting '94 (The Glory of the Latter Rain)	$45.00	
	VIDEOS		
	Campmeeting '94 Teaching Videos Morning Sessions, 10 Videos	$150.00	
	SUBTOTAL		
	SHIPPING (see chart)		
	TOTAL		

COMPLETE REVERSE SIDE FOR MAIL ORDER.

We will process your order upon receipt. We ask that you fill out all the information requested. Please allow two to three weeks for delivery. If there is ever a problem with a tape, please send it back to us with a note and we will replace it promptly.

THANK YOU FOR YOUR ORDER!

SHIPPING & HANDLING

Up to $12.00	$2.00
$12.01-$24.00	$2.95
$24.01-$49.99	$4.50
$50.00-$74.99	$6.50
$75.00-$99.00	$7.95
$99.01-$149.00	$9.95
over $149.00	$11.95

TYPE OF PAYMENT

Check ___   Charge ___   Visa ____   MasterCard ____   Discover ____

Credit Card # _____

Exp. Date_____

Please make checks payable to GABRIEL HEYMANS MINISTRIES
1500 Beville Rd., 606-256, Daytona Beach, FL 32114 • Phone 904/677-4410

PHONE ORDERS CALL 800/823-8829
FAX ORDERS CALL 904/677-7661

NAME _____

ADDRESS _____

CITY _____ STATE_____ ZIP _____

PHONE (_____)_____